Analysis of Changes in Water-Level Dynamics at Selected Sites in the Florida Everglades

By Paul A. Conrads and Stephen T. Benedict

Prepared as part of the U.S. Geological Survey Greater Everglades Priority Ecosystem Science

Scientific Investigations Report 2012–5286

U.S. Department of the Interior
U.S. Geological Survey

U.S. Department of the Interior
KEN SALAZAR, Secretary

U.S. Geological Survey
Marcia K. McNutt, Director

U.S. Geological Survey, Reston, Virginia: 2013

For more information on the USGS—the Federal source for science about the Earth, its natural and living resources, natural hazards, and the environment, visit http://www.usgs.gov or call 1-888-ASK-USGS

For an overview of USGS information products, including maps, imagery, and publications, visit http://www.usgs.gov/pubprod

To order this and other USGS information products, visit http://store.usgs.gov

Suggested citation:
Conrads, P.A., and Benedict, S.T., 2013, Analysis of changes in water-level dynamics at selected sites in the Florida Everglades: U.S. Geological Survey Scientific Investigations Report 2012–5286, 36 p.

Contents

Abstract...1

Introduction...1

    Purpose and Scope 3

    Description of Study Area 3

Approach...3

    Cumulative Z-Score...5

    Site Selection...7

    Period of Analysis 8

Results of Analysis of Water-Level Data...8

    Analysis for Period of Record 8

        Water Conservation Area 1..8

        Water Conservation Area 2..11

        Water Conservation Area 3..16

        Everglades National Park...18

    Analysis of Concurrent Period...18

    Comparison of Time Series Water-Level Data Among Sites 24

Summary..27

Selected References...28

Appendix. Overview of the Z-scores for Everglades Breakpoint Analysis Application.................29

Figures

1. Map showing locations of Water Conservation Areas and National Parks, Refuges, and Preserves in the Florida Everglades 2

2. Vegetation map of southern Florida, circa 1943 4

3. Map showing locations of water-level gages used in this study with respect to the Aquatic Cycling of Mercury in the Everglades sites....................................6

4. Daily water-level data at Site 64 in Water Conservation Area 3A for the period April 6, 1962, to December 31, 2011 7

5. Cumulative Z-score curve and daily water-level data and cumulative water-level frequency distribution curves for Site 64 in Water Conservation Area 3A for the period April 6, 1962, to December 31, 2011 7

6. Cumulative Z-score curve and daily water-level data and cumulative water-level frequency distribution curves for Site 7 in Water Conservation Area 1 for the period January 1, 1954, to December 31, 2011....................10

7. Cumulative Z-score curve and daily water-level data and cumulative water-level frequency distribution curves for Site 17 in Water Conservation Area 2A for the period June 10, 1952, to December 31, 2011.....................13

8. Cumulative Z-score curve and daily water-level data and cumulative water-level frequency distribution curves for Site 99 in Water Conservation Area 2B for the period July 12, 1991, to December 31, 2011......................15

9. Cumulative Z-score curve and daily water-level data and cumulative water-level frequency distribution curves for station 3ANE in Water Conservation Area 3A for the period October 12, 1978, to December 31, 2011 17

10 Cumulative Z-score curve and daily water-level data and cumulative water-level frequency distribution curves for station P37 in the Everglades National Park for the period January 15, 1953, to December 31, 2011..........21

11. Cumulative Z-score curve and daily water-level data and cumulative water-level frequency distribution curves for Site 7 in Water Conservation Area 1 for the period October 12, 1978, to December 31, 2011 22

12. Cumulative Z-score curve and daily water-level data and cumulative water-level frequency distribution curves for Site 17 in Water Conservation Area 2A for the period October 12, 1978, to December 31, 2011 22

13. Cumulative Z-score curve and daily water-level data and cumulative water-level frequency distribution curves for Site 64 in Water Conservation Area 3A for the period October 12, 1978, to December 31, 2011 23

14. Cumulative Z-score curve and daily water-level data and cumulative water-level frequency distribution curves for station P37 in Water Conservation Area 3A for the period October 12, 1978, to December 31, 2011 23

15. Cumulative Z-score curves and water-level data for selected water-level gages in the Florida Everglades for the period October 12, 1978, to December 31, 2011 25

16. Relation of the average 5th to 95th percentile water levels with respect to the 10 periods of analysis for selected gages in the Florida Everglades for the period October 12, 1978, to December 31, 2011 25

17. Relation of the difference between the average 5th to 95th percentile water level for the 10 periods of analysis and that of the full concurrent period for selected gages in the Florida Everglades 25

18. Relation of the Z-score for the average 5th to 95th percentile water levels with respect to the 10 periods of analysis for selected gages in the Florida Everglades 26

19. Range of water-level fluctuation based on the average 5th to 95th percentile water levels for the 10 periods of analysis at selected gages in the Florida Everglades 26

20. Largest increase in water level between consecutive periods based on the average 5th to 95th percentile water levels for the 10 periods of analysis at selected gages in the Florida Everglades 26

21. Largest decrease in water level between consecutive periods based on the average 5th to 95th percentile water levels for the 10 periods of analysis at selected gages in the Florida Everglades 27

Tables

1. List of ACME sites and corresponding water-level gages used to assess historical changes in hydrologic behavior..8

2. Selected statistics for the cumulative water-level frequency distribution curves for selected time periods at Site 7 in Water Conservation Area 1 in the Florida Everglades..9

3. Selected statistics for the cumulative water–level frequency distribution curves for selected time periods at Site 17 in Water Conservation Area 2A in the Florida Everglades..12

4. Selected statistics for the cumulative water–level frequency distribution curves for selected time periods at Site 99 in Water Conservation Area 2B in the Florida Everglades..14

5. Selected statistics for the cumulative water–level frequency distribution curves for selected time periods at Site 3ANE in Water Conservation Area 3A in the Florida Everglades..16

6. Selected statistics for the cumulative water–level frequency distribution curves for selected time periods at Site 64 in Water Conservation Area 3A in the Florida Everglades..19

7. Selected statistics for the cumulative water–level frequency distribution curves for selected time periods at station P37 in Water Conservation Area 3A in the Florida Everglades..20

Conversion Factors

Inch/Pound to SI

Multiply	By	To obtain
mile (mi)	1.609	kilometer (km)
square mile (mi^2)	2.590	square kilometer (km^2)

Horizontal coordinate information is referenced to North American Datum of 1983 (NAD 83).

Vertical coordinate information is referenced to North American Datum of 1988 (NAVD 88) or National Geodetic Vertical Datum of 1929 (NGVD 29).

Analysis of Changes in Water-Level Dynamics at Selected Sites in the Florida Everglades

By Paul A. Conrads and Stephen T. Benedict

Abstract

The historical modification and regulation of the hydrologic patterns in the Florida Everglades have resulted in changes in the ecosystem of South Florida and the Florida Everglades. Since the 1970s, substantial focus has been given to the restoration of the Everglades ecosystem. The U.S. Geological Survey through its Greater Everglades Priority Ecosystem Science and National Water-Quality Assessment Programs has been providing scientific information to resource managers to assist in the Everglades restoration efforts. The current investigation included development of a simple method to identify and quantify changes in historical hydrologic behavior within the Everglades that could be used by researchers to identify responses of ecological communities to those changes. Such information then could be used by resource managers to develop appropriate water-management practices within the Everglades to promote restoration. The identification of changes in historical hydrologic behavior within the Everglades was accomplished by analyzing historical time-series water-level data from selected gages in the Everglades using (1) break-point analysis of cumulative Z-scores to identify hydrologic changes and (2) cumulative water-level frequency distribution curves to evaluate the magnitude of those changes. This analytical technique was applied to six long-term water-level gages in the Florida Everglades. The break-point analysis for the concurrent period of record (1978–2011) identified 10 common periods of changes in hydrologic behavior at the selected gages. The water-level responses at each gage for the 10 periods displayed similarity in fluctuation patterns, highlighting the interconnectedness of the Florida Everglades hydrologic system. While the patterns were similar, the analysis also showed that larger fluctuations in water levels between periods occurred in Water Conservation Areas 2 and 3 in contrast to those in Water Conservation Area 1 and the Everglades National Park. Results from the analysis indicate that the cumulative Z-score curve, in conjunction with cumulative water-level frequency distribution curves, can be a useful tool in identifying and quantifying changes in historical hydrologic behavior within the Everglades. In addition to the analysis, a spreadsheet application was developed to assist in applying these techniques to time-series water-level data at gages within the Everglades and is included with this report.

Introduction

From the mid-1800s to the late 1900s, the hydrologic conditions of the Florida Everglades (hereinafter, referred to as the Everglades) have been substantially altered by the extensive draining of wetlands, diversion of natural flows, and regulation of natural flow patterns (fig. 1). These altered hydrologic patterns have produced commensurate environmental effects, such as lowered water tables, saltwater intrusion into freshwater aquifers, land subsidence, and altered water quality associated with agriculture and urban land-use practices. Of particular concern are the shifts in select populations of native and non-native plant and animal communities (McPherson and others, 1995). Since the 1970s, focus has been given to mitigate these adverse effects and, where possible, to begin restoration of the ecosystem and ecological communities of the Everglades. The U.S. Geological Survey (USGS) through its USGS Priority Ecosystem Science Program (*http://access.usgs.gov/*, accessed August 25, 2012) and National Water-Quality Assessment (NAWQA) Program (*http://water.usgs.gov/nawqa/*, accessed August 25, 2012) has been involved in data collection, data management, and field investigations within the Everglades, with a primary objective to provide scientific information to resource managers to assist in the mitigation and restoration process. A description of USGS activities in the Everglades can be found at the South Florida Information Access Web page: *http://sofia.usgs.gov/index.html* (accessed July 9, 2012).

The ecological communities of the Everglades are influenced by the current and historical hydrologic conditions. Small changes in seasonal and annual water levels can cause changes within those communities. The Everglades were originally a precipitation-driven hydrologic system, but the system is now heavily regulated. To promote restoration within the Everglades, it is important to understand how ecological communities respond to temporal and spatial changes in hydrology so that regulatory patterns can be used to promote hydrologic conditions that yield favorable responses. One method to evaluate the response of ecological communities to changes in hydrologic behavior is by review of historical responses. If periods of similar hydrologic behavior can be identified in historical gage records and associated with responses from ecological communities, then insights regarding hydrologic conditions that promote favorable or adverse responses can be identified and used in restoration efforts. A primary task of this investigation was to develop a simple method to identify changes in historical hydrologic behavior within the Everglades that could be used by researchers to identify responses of ecological communities to those changes.

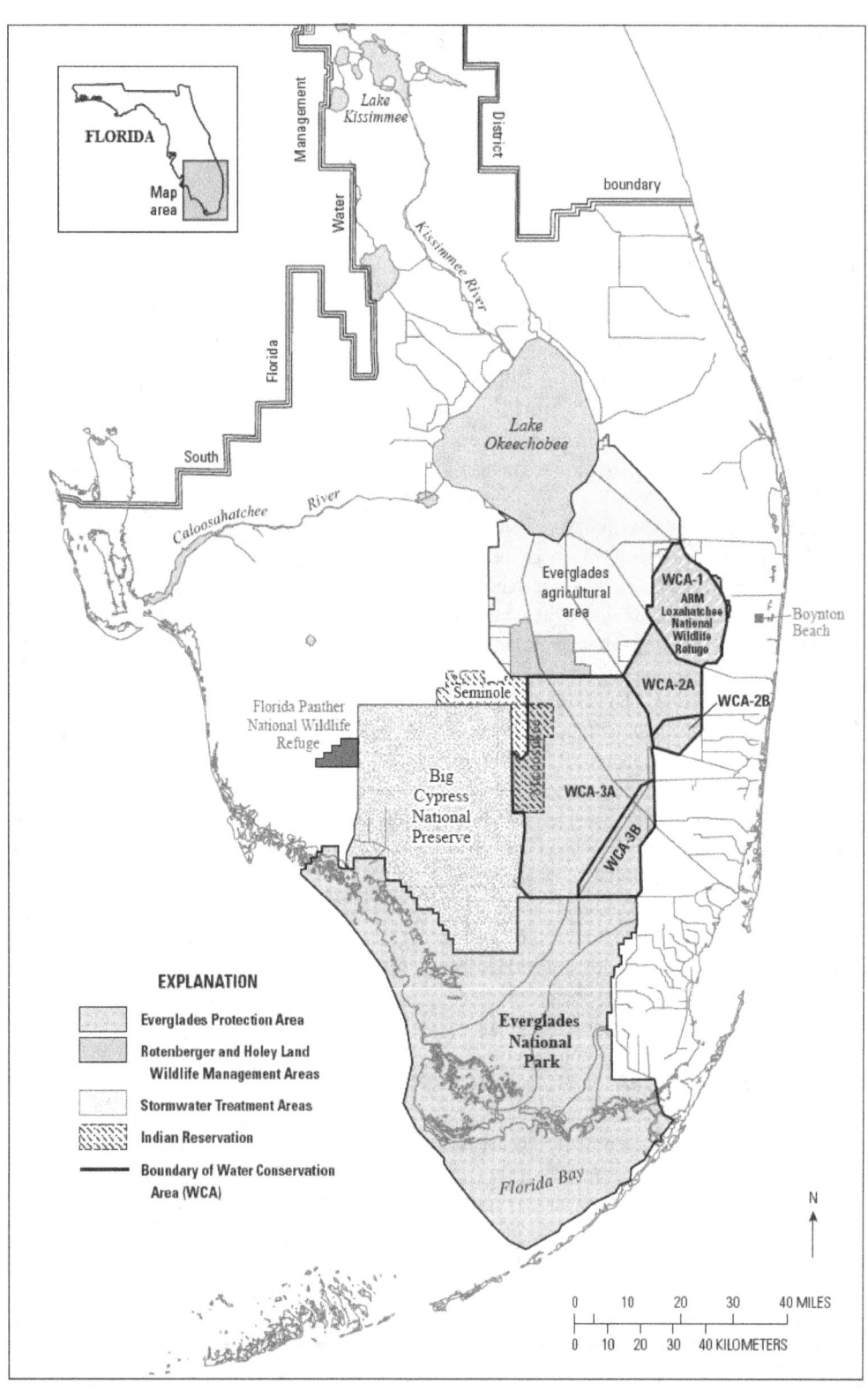

Figure 1.   Locations of Water Conservation Areas and National Parks, Refuges, and Preserves in the Florida Everglades (modified from U.S. Fish and Wildlife Service, 2000).

Purpose and Scope

The purpose of this report is to present the techniques and results of an investigation that included analyses of historical water-level (gage height) dynamics at six sites in the Florida Everglades in order to identify changes in historical hydrologic behavior. The geographical extent of the report is from Water Conservation Area 1 to the Everglades National Park (fig. 1). The analytical techniques included break-point analysis associated with cumulative Z-score curves to identify changes in hydrologic behavior and cumulative water-level frequency distribution curves to quantify those changes. Additionally, this report documents the Z-scores for Everglades Breakpoint Analysis (ZEBRA), a spreadsheet application developed to assist in applying the analytical techniques used in the investigation that also can be used to analyze other gages within the Everglades.

An important role of the USGS mission is to provide scientific information for the effective management of the Nation's water resources. The techniques presented in this report demonstrate how existing databases of continuous time-series data can be compiled and analyzed to assist researchers and resource managers to better understand complex natural systems and, therefore, better manage the resources of those systems. In particular, these techniques demonstrate how break-point analysis with cumulative Z-scores in combination with cumulative frequency distribution curves can be used to assess historical changes in a hydrologic system and the magnitude of those changes. The techniques are readily applicable to other natural systems for evaluation of historical time-series data.

Description of Study Area

The Everglades is a vast wetland consisting of approximately 2.9 million acres covering much of southern Florida (fig. 1). The Everglades primarily consists of peat soils and tall sawgrass that are interspersed with slightly raised tree islands covered by shrubs and woody vegetation (fig. 2; McPherson and others, 1995). Historically, the Everglades were an uninterrupted wetland that extended from Lake Okeechobee and flowed to the southwestern tip of Florida (Richardson and others, 1990). During the annual wet season (May or June to September or October), water levels would rise and inundate most of the land, producing seasonal flows into the Florida Bay and the Gulf of Mexico. In contrast, during the dry season, water levels declined and were near land surface (McPherson and others, 1995). This hydrologic pattern helped produce and sustain the unique ecosystem of the Everglades.

From the mid-1800s to the late 1900s, the flow patterns, and thus the ecosystem, of the Everglades have been substantially altered. Beginning in the mid-1800s, wetlands began to be drained and used for agricultural purposes and urban development such that by the early 1990s, about 50 percent of the historic Everglades had been drained (McPherson and others, 1995). With population growth and increased agricultural production, flood mitigation and water use in South Florida became prominent concerns. To address those concerns, Water Conservation Areas (WCAs) 1, 2, and 3 (fig. 1) were constructed by the U.S. Army Corps of Engineers in the 1940s with the goal of regulating water through an extensive series of levees and canals. In general, the WCAs store water during the wet season and supply water during the dry season. The combined effect of drained wetlands and water regulation introduced during the 1800s and 1900s diverts an estimated 40 percent of the water originally flowing through the Everglades (McPherson and others, 1995). The substantial changes in land use and flow patterns within the Everglades have had adverse environmental effects on the hydrology, water quality, and native plant and animal communities (McPherson and others, 1995). Since the late 1900s, through the collaboration of Federal, State, and private agencies, substantial focus has been given to mitigate these adverse effects and, where possible, to begin restoration of the ecosystem and ecological communities of the Everglades.

Approach

Correlating the response of ecological communities to changes in hydrologic behavior is requisite for evaluating best-management practices for water regulation and restoration efforts within the Everglades. The focus of this investigation was to develop a simple method to identify and quantify historical hydrologic changes that, in turn, could be used by researchers to make such correlations. The primary data source for evaluating historical changes in hydrologic behavior within the Everglades is the extensive water-level gage networks in WCAs 1, 2, and 3, Big Cypress National Preserve, and the Everglades National Park (fig. 1) maintained by State and Federal Agencies. Some of the gages have data from as long ago as the 1930s. The data from the water-level monitoring sites used in this report are part of the Everglades Depth Estimation Network (EDEN), a subset of more than 250 water-level gages maintained by Big Cypress National Preserve, Everglades National Park, South Florida Water Management District, and the USGS (Telis, 2006).

Changes in hydrologic behavior within the Everglades can be subtle and difficult to discern within these water-level data; therefore, analytical tools must be used to identify such changes. A proven technique for identifying subtle changes, or break points, in time-series data is the use of the cumulative Z-score curve (Buishand, 1982; Rodionov, 2005; Briceño and others, 2010). While there are more rigorous mathematical techniques to investigate changes in time-series data (Buishand, 1982; Rodionov, 2005), the cumulative Z-score curve provides a simple graphical method in which abrupt changes in the slope (break points) of the cumulative curve indicate potential changes in the behavior of the system. This analytical technique, in conjunction with cumulative

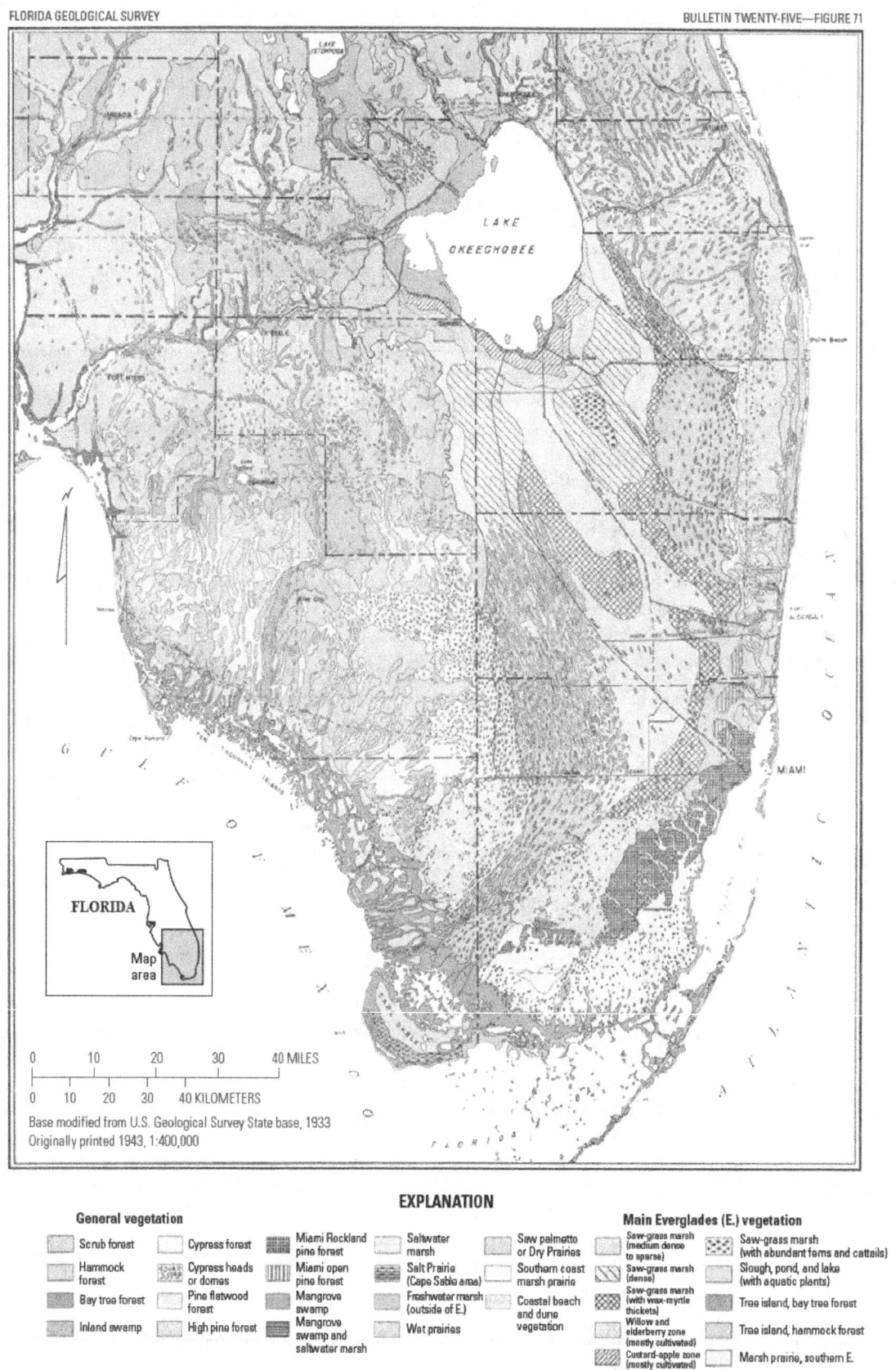

FLORIDA GEOLOGICAL SURVEY

BULLETIN TWENTY-FIVE—FIGURE 71

EXPLANATION

General vegetation

Scrub forest

Hammock forest

Bay tree forest

Inland swamp

Cypress forest

Cypress heads or domes

Pine flatwood forest

High pine forest

Miami Rockland pine forest

Miami open pine forest

Mangrove swamp

Mangrove swamp and saltwater marsh

Saltwater marsh

Salt Prairie (Cape Sable area)

Freshwater marsh (outside of E.)

Wet prairies

Saw palmetto or Dry Prairies

Southern coast marsh prairie

Coastal beach and dune vegetation

Main Everglades (E.) vegetation

Saw-grass marsh (medium dense to sparse)

Saw-grass marsh (dense)

Saw-grass marsh (with wax-myrtle thickets)

Willow and elderberry zone (mostly cultivated)

Custard-apple zone (mostly cultivated)

Saw-grass marsh (with abundant ferns and cattails)

Slough, pond, and lake (with aquatic plants)

Tree island, bay tree forest

Tree island, hammock forest

Marsh prairie, southern E.

Figure 2.   Vegetation map of southern Florida, circa 1943 (modified from Davis, 1943).

frequency distribution curves (Iman and Conover, 1983), was applied to time-series water-level data from selected gages in the Everglades in order to identify and quantify changes in hydrologic behavior. A spreadsheet application was developed to assist in applying the technique and is documented in the appendix. A description of this technique and example of its application follows.

Cumulative Z-Score

For a given set of data with n measurements, a Z-score (Z_i; eq. 1) is the measured value (X_i) minus the mean value ($\bar{X}$; eq. 2) divided by the standard deviation (s; eq. 3) and defines how many standard deviations the measured value is above or below the mean (Iman and Conover, 1983).

$$Z_i = (X_i - \bar{X})/s \qquad (1)$$

$$\bar{X} = \sum_{i=1}^{n} \frac{X_i}{n} \qquad (2)$$

$$s = \sqrt{\sum_{i=1}^{n} \frac{(X_i - \bar{X})^2}{(n-1)}} \qquad (3)$$

The cumulative Z-score curve is determined by calculating a cumulative total of the Z-scores with respect to time and represents the cumulative sum of the deviations from the mean. Changes in the slope of the cumulative Z-score curve indicate that the mean for a subset of the dataset deviates from the mean for the period of record and thus indicates a change in the behavior, or dynamics, of the time-series data. Positive slopes along the cumulative Z-score curve represent a subset of the data that has a mean greater than the mean for the period of record. Similarly, negative slopes represent a subset of the data that has a mean lower than the mean for the period of record. Slopes with a value of zero represent a subset of the data that has a mean equal to the mean for the period of record (Buishand, 1982).

For example, a 50-year daily water-level time series for Site 64 (fig. 3) is shown in figure 4. One can see that there is a difference in the hydrologic behavior before and after 1990, but changes within these periods are more difficult to discern. The Z-score for each day was computed and the cumulative Z-score curve plotted (fig. 5A). The cumulative Z-score curve shows eight substantial breaks (marked by red vertical lines), or changes, in the slope of the line occurring in the following years: 1966, 1971, 1977, 1988, 1992, 2000, 2001, and 2006. (The small annual changes are due to wet- and dry-season water-level differences.) The break points in the cumulative Z-score curve are indicative of changes in the hydrologic behavior at Site 64 resulting from changes in climatic and (or) water regulation patterns. A comparison of the mean water level to the time-series water-level data between break points (also called periods) in figure 5A demonstrates how the slope of the cumulative Z-score curve indicates whether the mean water-level data for that period is above, below, or near the mean for the period of record. For the period of 1962 to 1966, the slope of the cumulative Z-score curve is negative, and most of the data for that period are below the mean water level. For the period of 1977 to 1988, the slope of the cumulative Z-score curve is relatively flat, and the data for that period are scattered about the mean water level. For the period of 1992 to 2000, the slope of the cumulative Z-score curve is positive, and most of the data for that period are above the mean water level.

To evaluate the relative differences of water levels during the nine periods identified by the break-point analysis, cumulative water-level frequency distribution curves can be developed for each period (fig. 5B). Selected statistical values, such as the mean, standard deviation, 50th percentile, and the average of the 5th to 95th percentiles associated with the cumulative frequency distribution curves of figure 5B can be computed in order to evaluate the relative change in water level between the periods. (Note: The average of the 5th to 95th percentiles was calculated by taking percentiles for the data in each period in 1-percent increments and then averaging the percentiles between 5 and 95, inclusive.) Tabulations of these statistics are presented as part of the analysis for each gage.

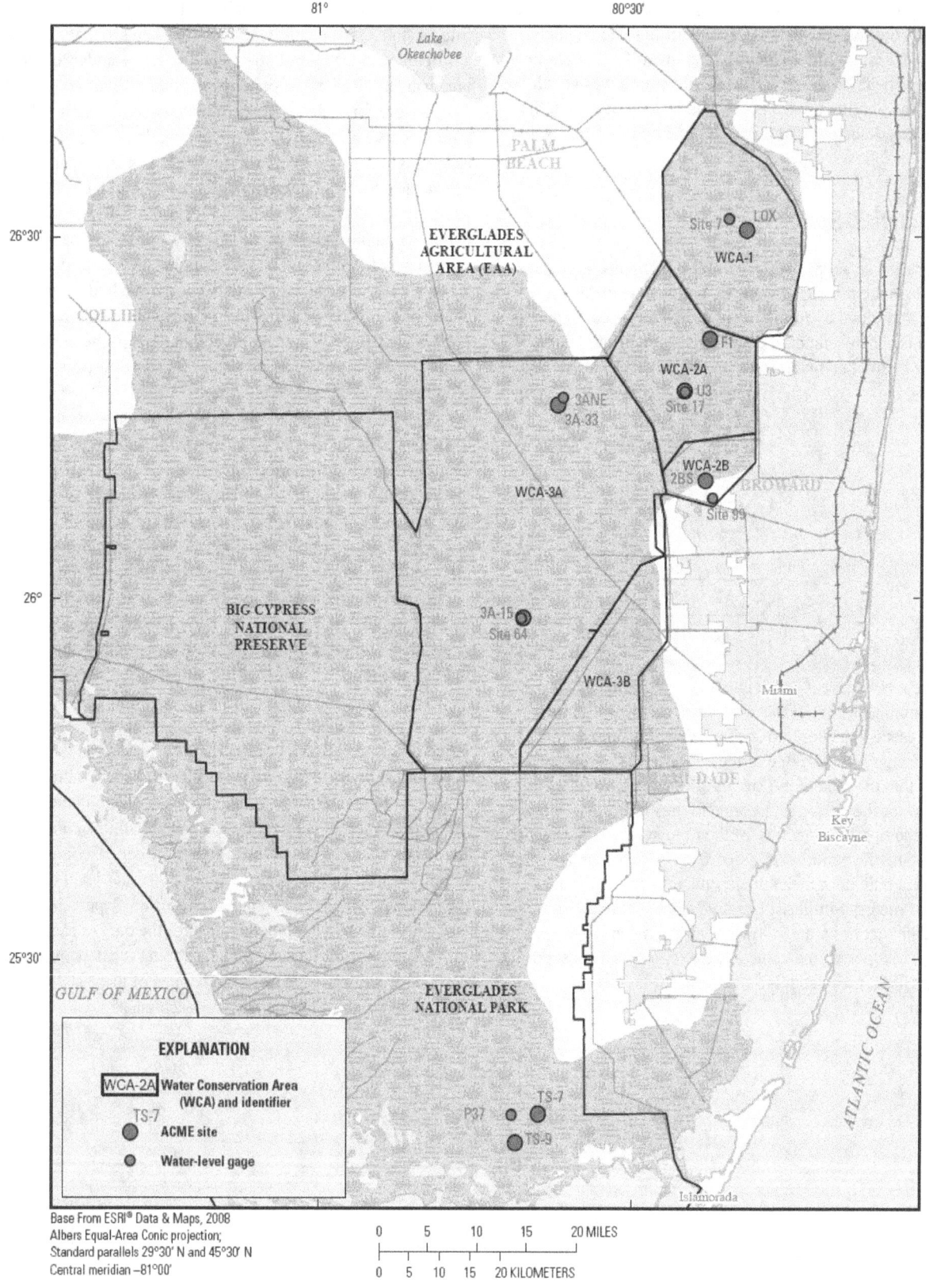

Figure 3. Locations of water-level gages used in this study with respect to the Aquatic Cycling of Mercury in the Everglades (ACME) sites.

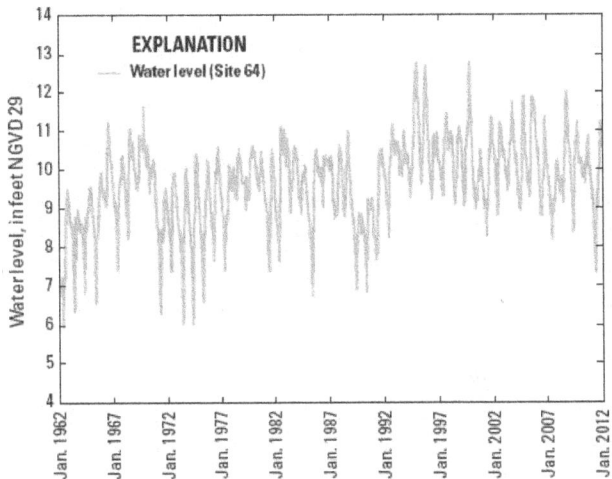

Figure 4.   Daily water-level data at Site 64 in Water Conservation Area 3A for the period April 6, 1962, to December 31, 2011.

Site Selection

Long-term water-level gages close to sampling sites for the Aquatic Cycling of Mercury in the Everglades (ACME) Project were identified for inclusion in the analysis. In 1994, a consortium of agencies lead by the USGS began the ACME Project to study the factors contributing to high levels of mercury in the Everglades (*http://sofia.usgs.gov/projects/index.php?project_url=evergl_merc*, accessed June 25, 2012). The overall objective is to understand mercury cycling well enough to create management strategies that will minimize bioaccumulation in the Everglades (Krabbenhoft and others, 2000). One aspect of the ACME investigation is the assessment of how changes in hydrologic behavior may affect the mercury cycle within the Everglades. To assist the ACME investigation with this assessment, the current investigation included analyses of changes in hydrologic behavior at six long-term water-level gages in close proximity to the ACME sampling sites (fig. 3; table 1). Sites having longer periods of record were given a higher preference in the selection process. Often, monitoring stations in the Everglades have been maintained under different, although similar, station names. In this report, the water-level station names are consistent with those used in the EDEN network.

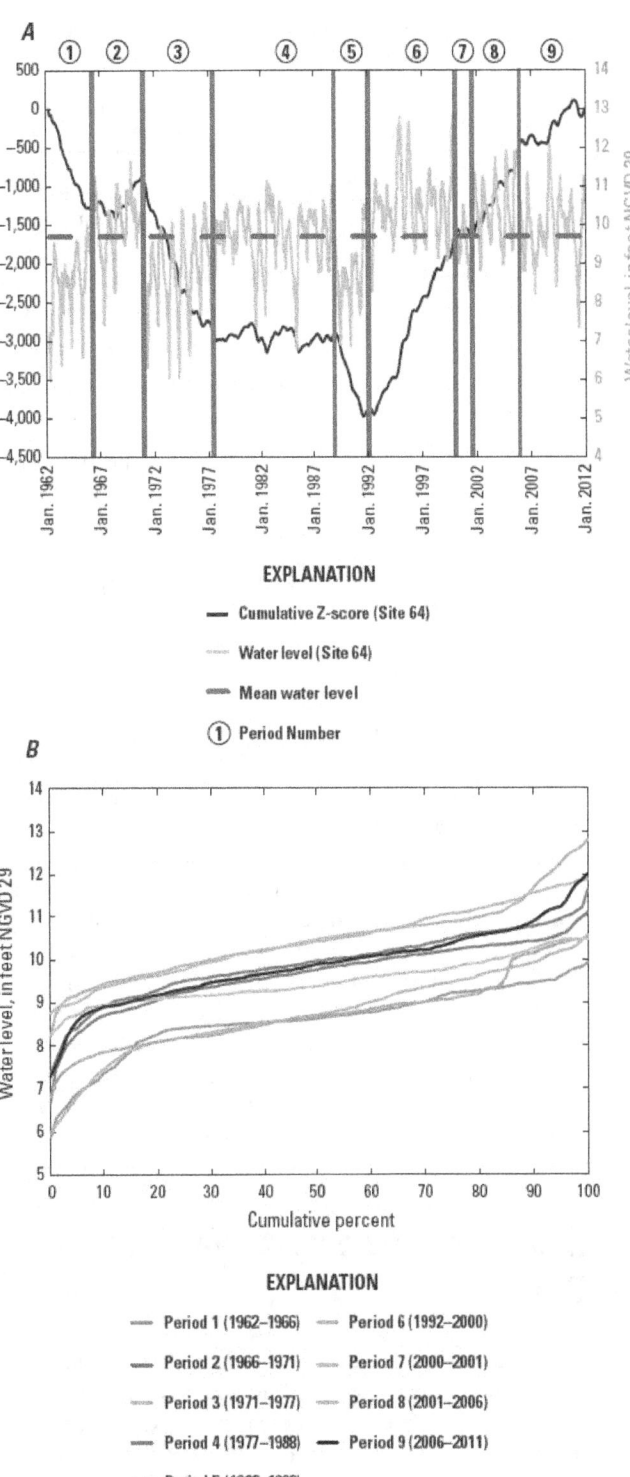

Figure 5.   (*A*) Cumulative Z-score curve and daily water-level data and (*B*) cumulative water-level frequency distribution curves for Site 64 in Water Conservation Area 3A for the period April 6, 1962, to December 31, 2011.

Table 1.   List of ACME sites and corresponding water-level gages used to assess historical changes in hydrologic behavior.

[ACME, Aquatic Cycling of Mercury in the Everglades project; DMS, degrees, minutes, and seconds; WCA, Water Conservation Area; ENP, Everglades National Park]

ACME site (see fig. 3 for site location)	Basin	*Corresponding water-level gage	Latitude of gage, in DMS	Longitude of gage, in DMS	Period of record for gage	
					Start date (year)	End date (year)
LOX	WCA-1	Site 7	263111	802049	1954	2011
F1	WCA-2A	Site 17	261712	802439	1952	2011
U3	WCA-2A	Site 17	261712	802439	1952	2011
2BS	WCA-2B	Site 99	260821	802202	1991	2011
3A-33	WCA-3A	3ANE	261644	803617	1978	2011
3A-15	WCA-3A	Site 64	255832	804009	1962	2011
TS-7	ENP	P37	251703	804118	1953	2011
TS-9	ENP	P37	251703	804118	1953	2011

*Often, monitoring stations in the Everglades have been maintained under different, although similar, station names. In this report, the station names are consistent with those used in the Everglades Depth Estimation Network (EDEN; Telis, 2006).

Period of Analysis

The selected water-level gages for this investigation have periods of record ranging from 21 to 60 years (table 1). In order to understand the hydrologic trends at each site, the break-point analysis associated with the cumulative Z-score curves was applied to each of the six water-level gages for the period of record. Additionally, to discern the differences and similarities in hydrologic behavior between the selected gages, the break-point analysis was applied to each gage for a concurrent period of time between October 12, 1978, and December 31, 2011. The period of record for Site 99 is from July 12, 1991, to December 31, 2011; while this record is shorter than that used in the concurrent period analysis (October 12, 1978, to December 31, 2011), it was still included in that analysis for information.

Results of Analysis of Water-Level Data

Data for the selected water-level gages were compiled in the spreadsheet application, ZEBRA, in order to develop the cumulative Z-score curves for each gage. Each curve for the respective water-level gage was reviewed to identify changes in the slope (break points) of the cumulative curve indicating potential changes in the hydrologic behavior. Some slope break points were more pronounced than others requiring judgment in the selection of some of the break points. The cumulative Z-score curves for the respective gages often had common break points, and where possible, the same break points were chosen to allow comparisons between gages. In some cases, the slope change in the cumulative Z-score curve was less pronounced at a given gage than at the other gages,

but the same break point was still chosen. The ZEBRA spreadsheet application only allows nine break points; therefore, nine or fewer break points were identified for each curve. Having identified break points for the cumulative Z-score curve for each gage, cumulative frequency distribution curves for water level were developed for the time periods between the break points. (Note: The break-point dates were entered into ZEBRA, and the cumulative frequency distribution curves for a given period were automatically generated in the spreadsheet.) This process was applied to the water-level data at each gage for both the period of record and for the concurrent period of October 12, 1978, to December 31, 2011, and results are presented in the following sections.

Analysis for Period of Record

The cumulative Z-score curves and cumulative frequency distribution curves for the period of record associated with the water-level gages listed in table 1 are presented in this section in upstream to downstream order.

Water Conservation Area 1

Site 7 is located in WCA-1 (fig. 3) and has a 58-year period of record from 1954 to 2011 (table 1) with a mean water level of 16.12 ft (table 2). For the period of record, water levels were lowest during period 6 (1988–1991) with a mean of 15.41 ft, and highest during period 7 (1991–2000) with a mean of 16.55 ft (fig. 6; table 2). The largest increasing shift in water levels between subsequent periods occurred between periods 6 and 7 (1988–1991 and 1991–2000, respectively) with a value of 1.14 ft based on the mean (table 2). The largest decreasing shift in water levels between subsequent periods occurred between periods 5 and 6 (1982–1988 and 1988–1991, respectively) with a value of –0.97 ft based on the mean (table 2).

Table 2. Selected statistics for the cumulative water-level frequency distribution curves for selected time periods at Site 7 in Water Conservation Area 1 in the Florida Everglades.

[NGVD 29, National Geodetic Vertical Datum of 1929]

Period	Start date	End date	Number of observations	Standard deviation, in feet	Mean, in feet NGVD 29	50th Percentile water level, in feet NGVD 29	Average 5th–95th percentile water level, in feet NGVD 29	Change from previous period		
								Mean, in feet	50th Percentile water level, in feet	Average 5th–95th percentile water level, in feet
Period of Record—Janurary 1, 1954, to December 31, 2011										
1	January 1, 1954	August 1, 1964	3,353	0.50	15.66	15.68	15.66			
2	August 1, 1964	June 1, 1970	2,131	0.57	16.20	16.21	16.21	0.54	0.53	0.55
3	June 1, 1970	August 1, 1973	1,158	0.70	15.63	15.70	15.65	−0.57	−0.51	−0.56
4	August 1, 1973	May 1, 1982	3,196	0.44	15.96	15.93	15.96	0.33	0.23	0.31
5	May 1, 1982	March 1, 1988	2,132	0.38	16.38	16.35	16.37	0.42	0.42	0.41
6	March 1, 1988	January 1, 1991	848	0.62	15.41	15.53	15.43	−0.97	−0.83	−0.94
7	January 1, 1991	January 1, 2000	3,220	0.47	16.55	16.51	16.54	1.14	0.99	1.10
8	January 1, 2000	December 31, 2011	4,378	0.47	16.38	16.43	16.39	−0.17	−0.08	−0.15
Record	January 1, 1954	December 31, 2011	20,410	0.61	16.12	16.15	16.13			
Concurrent Period—October 12, 1978, to December 31, 2011										
1	October 12, 1978	December 1, 1980	782	0.46	16.07	15.91	16.06			
2	December 1, 1980	June 1, 1982	548	0.33	15.76	15.76	15.75	−0.31	−0.15	−0.30
3	June 1, 1982	November 1, 1988	2,346	0.38	16.34	16.32	16.34	0.58	0.56	0.58
4	November 1, 1988	July 1, 1991	717	0.65	15.34	15.42	15.34	−1.00	−0.90	−0.99
5	July 1, 1991	August 1, 1994	1,128	0.38	16.34	16.33	16.34	1.00	0.91	1.00
6	August 1, 1994	January 1, 1996	519	0.52	16.79	16.80	16.77	0.45	0.47	0.42
7	January 1, 1996	February 1, 2000	1,493	0.44	16.65	16.60	16.64	−0.14	−0.20	−0.12
8	February 1, 2000	August 1, 2001	548	0.49	16.15	16.13	16.14	−0.50	−0.48	−0.50
9	August 1, 2001	March 1, 2004	944	0.35	16.62	16.63	16.62	0.47	0.50	0.48
10	March 1, 2004	December 31, 2011	2,857	0.47	16.34	16.39	16.36	−0.28	−0.24	−0.26
Record	October 12, 1978	December 31, 2011	11,873	0.55	16.31	16.35	16.32			

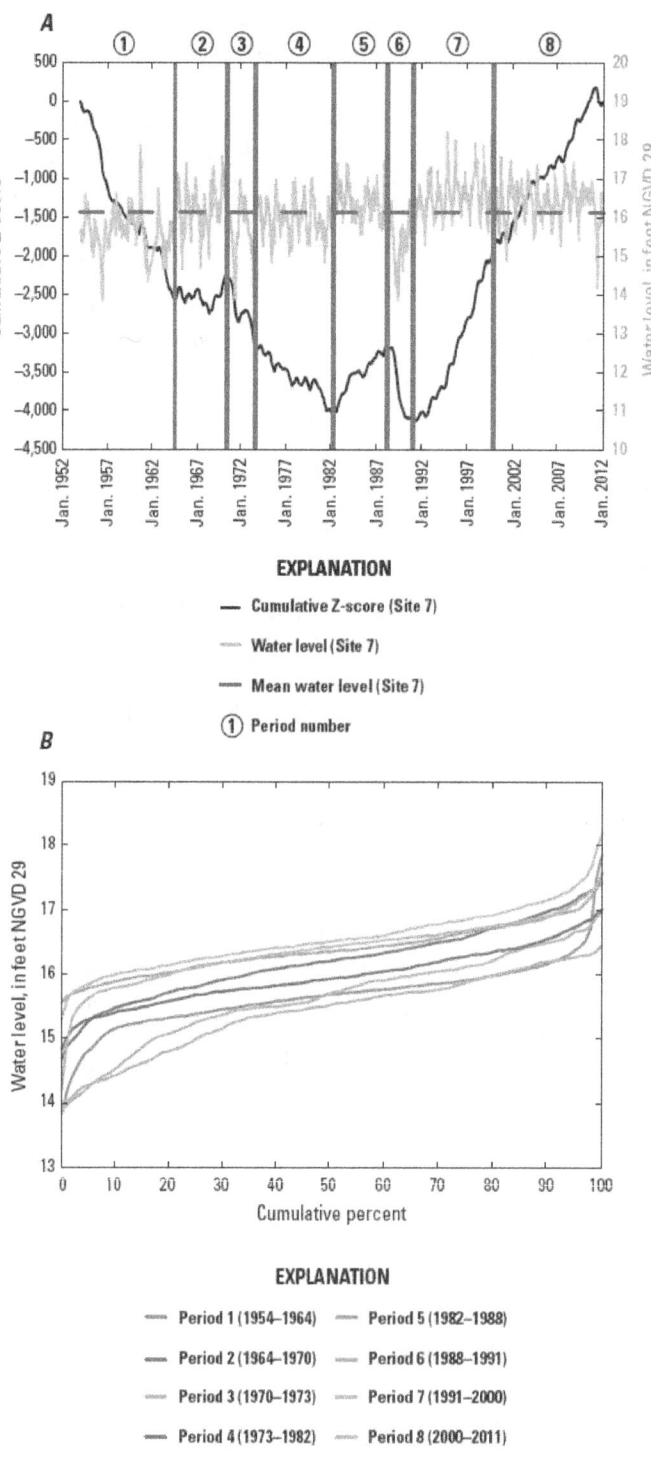

Figure 6. (*A*) Cumulative Z-score curve and daily water-level data and (*B*) cumulative water-level frequency distribution curves for Site 7 in Water Conservation Area 1 for the period January 1, 1954, to December 31, 2011.

Water Conservation Area 2

Site 17 is located in WCA-2A (fig. 3) and has a 60-year period of record from 1952 to 2011 (table 1) with a mean water level of 12.41 ft (table 3). For the period of record, water levels were lowest during period 1 (1952–1957) with a mean of 11.31 ft, and highest during period 5 (1975–1980) with a mean of 13.59 ft (fig. 7; table 3). The largest increasing shift in water levels between subsequent periods occurred between periods 2 and 3 (1957–1962 and 1962–1970, respectively) with a value of 1.51 ft based on the mean (table 3). The largest decreasing shift in water levels between subsequent periods occurred between periods 5 and 6 (1975–1980 and 1980–1994, respectively) with a value of −1.79 ft based on the mean (table 3). It is interesting to note that Sites 7 and 17 have a similar period of record (1954–2011 and 1952–2011,

respectively), but the periods of high and low water levels occur at different periods of time.

Site 99 is located in WCA-2B (fig. 3) and has a 21-year period of record from 1991–2011 (table 1) with a mean water level of 9.84 ft (table 4). For the period of record, water levels were lowest during period 1 (1991–1992) with a mean of 8.55 ft, and highest during period 3 (1994–1997) with a mean of 10.55 ft (fig. 8; table 4). The largest increasing shift in water levels between subsequent periods occurred between periods 6 and 7 (2006–2008 and 2008–2011, respectively) with a value of 1.38 ft based on the mean (table 4). The largest decreasing shift in water levels between subsequent periods occurred between periods 7 and 8 (2008–2011 and January 2011–December 2011, respectively) with a value of −1.36 ft based on the mean (table 4).

Table 3.   Selected statistics for the cumulative water-level frequency distribution curves for selected time periods at Site 17 in Water Conservation Area 2A in the Florida Everglades.

[NGVD 29, National Geodetic Vertical Datum of 1929]

Period	Start date	End date	Number of observations	Standard deviation, in feet	Mean, in feet NGVD 29	50th Percentile water level, in feet NGVD 29	Average 5th–95th percentile water level, in feet NGVD 29	Change from previous period		
								Mean, in feet	50th Percentile water level, in feet	Average 5th–95th percentile water level, in feet
Period of Record—June 10, 1952, to December 31, 2011										
1	June 10, 1952	May 1, 1957	1,423	0.76	11.31	11.35	11.32			
2	May 1, 1957	July 1, 1962	1,740	0.61	11.95	11.81	11.93	0.64	0.46	0.61
3	July 1, 1962	September 1, 1970	2,985	0.77	13.46	13.44	13.45	1.51	1.63	1.52
4	September 1, 1970	February 1, 1975	1,615	0.95	12.57	12.58	12.59	−0.89	−0.86	−0.86
5	February 1, 1975	December 1, 1980	2,131	0.64	13.59	13.59	13.62	1.02	1.01	1.03
6	December 1, 1980	March 1, 1994	4,839	0.75	11.80	11.71	11.80	−1.79	−1.88	−1.81
7	March 1, 1994	April 1, 1996	763	1.08	12.96	12.80	12.92	1.16	1.09	1.12
8	April 1, 1996	December 31, 2011	5,729	0.86	12.24	12.16	12.23	−0.72	−0.64	−0.69
Record	June 10, 1952	December 31, 2011	21,218	1.06	12.41	12.29	12.40			
Concurrent Period—October 12, 1978, to December 31, 2011										
1	October 12, 1978	December 1, 1980	782	0.67	13.80	13.73	13.80			
2	December 1, 1980	June 1, 1982	548	0.57	11.61	11.52	11.60	−2.19	−2.21	−2.20
3	June 1, 1982	November 1, 1988	2,346	0.68	11.88	11.72	11.86	0.27	0.21	0.26
4	November 1, 1988	July 1, 1991	973	0.75	11.33	11.41	11.35	−0.55	−0.31	−0.50
5	July 1, 1991	August 1, 1994	1,128	0.67	12.18	12.15	12.17	0.85	0.74	0.82
6	August 1, 1994	January 1, 1996	519	0.92	13.47	13.38	13.47	1.29	1.23	1.29
7	January 1, 1996	February 1, 2000	1,493	0.84	12.35	12.28	12.33	−1.12	−1.10	−1.14
8	February 1, 2000	August 1, 2001	548	0.59	11.86	11.80	11.84	−0.49	−0.48	−0.49
9	August 1, 2001	March 1, 2006	1,674	0.84	12.37	12.21	12.34	0.51	0.41	0.51
10	March 1, 2006	December 31, 2011	2,108	0.89	12.14	12.13	12.15	−0.23	−0.08	−0.20
Record	October 12, 1978	December 31, 2011	12,110	0.97	12.21	12.05	12.19			

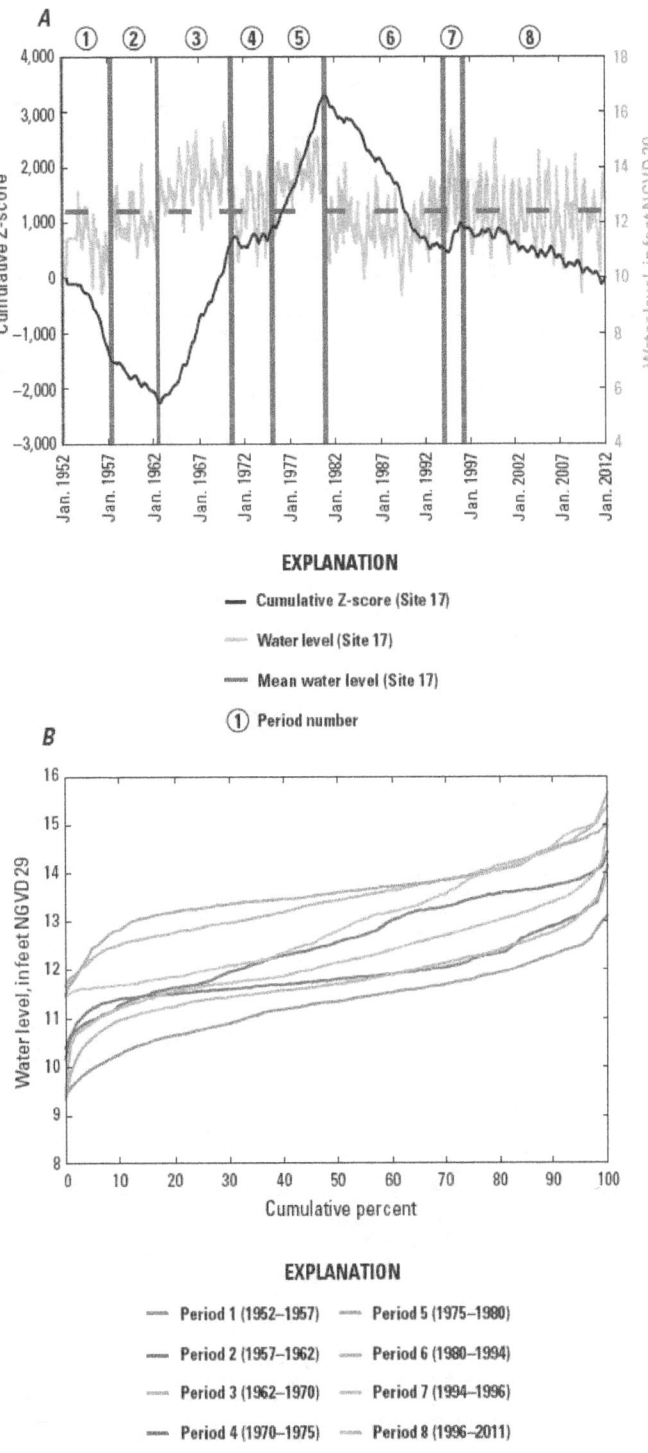

EXPLANATION

—— Cumulative Z-score (Site 17)

---- Water level (Site 17)

---- Mean water level (Site 17)

① Period number

EXPLANATION

—— Period 1 (1952–1957)   —— Period 5 (1975–1980)

—— Period 2 (1957–1962)   —— Period 6 (1980–1994)

—— Period 3 (1962–1970)   —— Period 7 (1994–1996)

—— Period 4 (1970–1975)   —— Period 8 (1996–2011)

Figure 7. (*A*) Cumulative Z-score curve and daily water-level data and (*B*) cumulative water-level frequency distribution curves for Site 17 in Water Conservation Area 2A for the period June 10, 1952, to December 31, 2011.

Table 4.   Selected statistics for the cumulative water-level frequency distribution curves for selected time periods at Site 99 in Water Conservation Area 2B in the Florida Everglades.

[NGVD 29, National Geodetic Vertical Datum of 1929]

									Change from previous period		
Period	Start date	End date	Number of observations	Standard deviation, in feet	Mean, in feet NGVD 29	50th Percentile water level, in feet NGVD 29	Average 5th–95th percentile water level, in feet NGVD 29	Mean, in feet	50th Percentile water level, in feet	Average 5th–95th percentile water level, in feet
Period of Record—July 12, 1991, to December 31, 2011**											
1	July 12, 1991	September 1, 1992	389	1.59	8.55	9.17	8.68			
2	September 1, 1992	August 1, 1994	684	0.76	9.86	9.96	9.88	1.31	0.79	1.19
3	August 1, 1994	January 1, 1997	870	0.57	10.55	10.63	10.54	0.69	0.67	0.66
4	January 1, 1997	January 1, 2001	1,399	0.82	10.31	10.58	10.37	−0.24	−0.05	−0.17
5	January 1, 2001	March 1, 2006	1,876	1.26	9.87	10.29	9.98	−0.44	−0.29	−0.39
6	March 1, 2006	August 1, 2008	879	1.39	8.88	9.18	8.98	−0.99	−1.11	−1.00
7	August 1, 2008	January 1, 2011	884	0.81	10.26	10.37	10.33	1.38	1.19	1.35
8	January 1, 2011	December 31, 2011	365	2.07	8.90	9.43	8.99	−1.36	−0.93	−1.35
Record	July 12, 1991	December 31, 2011	7,339	1.28	9.84	10.19	9.97			

** The period of record for the water-level gage at Site 99 is from July 12, 1991, to December 31, 2011. While this record is shorter than that used in the concurrent period analysis (October 12, 1978, to December 31, 2011), it was still included in the analysis for information.

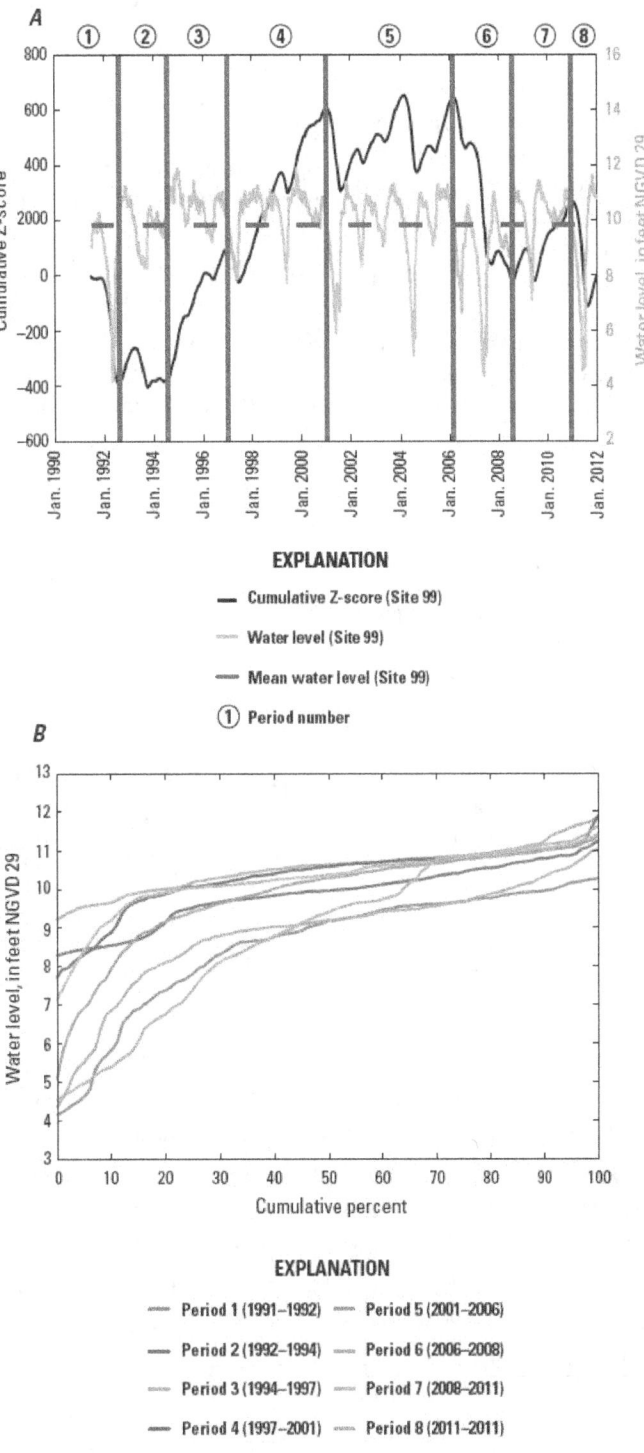

Figure 8. (*A*) Cumulative Z-score curve and daily water-level data and (*B*) cumulative water-level frequency distribution curves for Site 99 in Water Conservation Area 2B for the period July 12, 1991, to December 31, 2011.

Water Conservation Area 3

Water-level gage 3ANE is located in WCA-3A (fig. 3) and has a 34-year period of record from 1978–2011 (table 1) with a mean water level of 10.59 ft (table 5). The period of record (January 1, 1978, to December 31, 2011) and the concurrent period (October 12, 1978, to December 31, 2011) are similar, so only the concurrent period of analysis is presented. For the concurrent period of record, water levels were lowest during period 4 (1988–1991) with a mean of 8.84 ft, and highest during period 6 (1994–1996) with a mean of 12.05 ft (fig. 9; table 5). The largest increasing shift in water levels between subsequent periods occurred between periods 4 and 5 (1988–1991 and 1991–1994, respectively) with a value of 1.98 ft based on the mean (table 5). The largest decreasing shift in water levels between subsequent periods occurred

between periods 3 and 4 (1982–1988 and 1988–1991, respectively) with a value of –1.90 ft based on the mean (table 5).

Site 64 is located in WCA-3A (fig. 3) and has a 50-year period of record from 1962 to 2011 (table 1) with a mean water level of 9.68 ft (table 6). For the period of record, water levels were lowest during period 1 (1962–1966) with a mean of 8.63 ft, and highest during period 6 (1992–2000) with a mean of 10.49 ft (fig. 5; table 6). The largest increasing shift in water levels between subsequent periods occurred between periods 5 and 6 (1988–1992 and 1992–2000, respectively) with a value of 1.70 ft based on the mean (table 6). The largest decreasing shift in water levels between subsequent periods occurred between periods 2 and 3 (1966–1971 and 1971–1977, respectively) with a value of –1.15 ft based on the mean (table 6).

Table 5. Selected statistics for the cumulative water-level frequency distribution curves for selected time periods at Site 3ANE in Water Conservation Area 3A in the Florida Everglades.

[NGVD 29, National Geodetic Vertical Datum of 1929]

Period	Start date	End date	Number of observations	Standard deviation, in feet	Mean, in feet NGVD 29	50th Percentile water level, in feet NGVD 29	Average 5th–95th percentile water level, in feet NGVD 29	Change from previous period		
								Mean, in feet	50th Percentile water level, in feet	Average 5th–95th percentile water level, in feet
Concurrent period—October 12, 1978, to December 31, 2011										
1	October 12, 1978	December 1, 1980	729	0.42	10.44	10.54	10.46			
2	December 1, 1980	June 1, 1982	370	1.30	9.08	9.57	9.13	–1.36	–0.97	–1.34
3	June 1, 1982	November 1, 1988	2,146	0.66	10.74	10.78	10.77	1.66	1.22	1.64
4	November 1, 1988	July 1, 1991	940	1.30	8.84	9.00	8.86	–1.90	–1.79	–1.91
5	July 1, 1991	August 1, 1994	1,128	0.70	10.82	10.88	10.85	1.98	1.89	1.99
6	August 1, 1994	January 1, 1996	519	0.94	12.05	12.06	12.05	1.23	1.18	1.20
7	January 1, 1996	February 1, 2000	1,493	0.81	10.96	11.06	10.97	–1.09	–1.00	–1.09
8	February 1, 2000	August 1, 2001	466	0.51	10.39	10.47	10.39	–0.57	–0.60	–0.57
9	August 1, 2001	March 1, 2006	1,674	0.72	11.05	10.94	11.05	0.66	0.48	0.66
10	March 1, 2006	December 31, 2011	2,009	0.73	10.48	10.45	10.43	–0.57	–0.49	–0.62
Record	October 12, 1978	December 31, 2011	11,465	1.06	10.59	10.67	10.64			

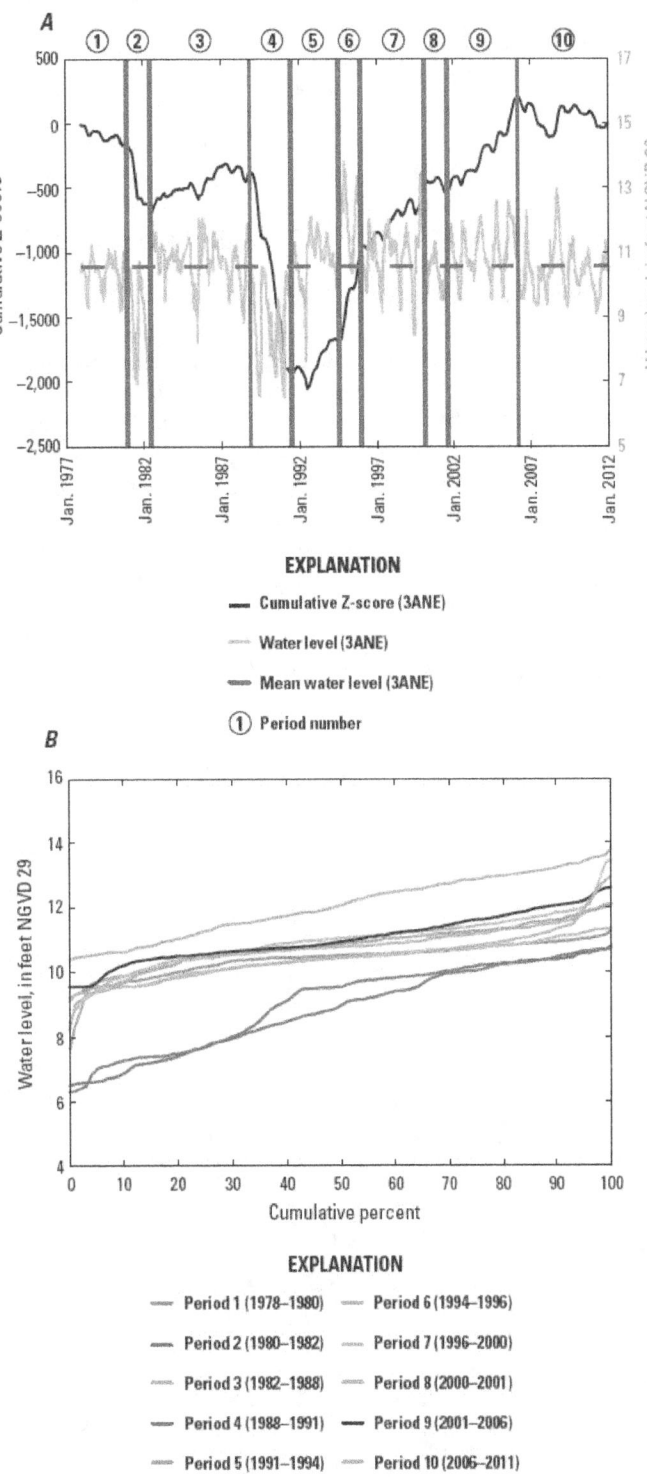

Figure 9.   (*A*) Cumulative Z-score curve and daily water-level data and (*B*) cumulative water-level frequency distribution curves for station 3ANE in Water Conservation Area 3A for the period October 12, 1978, to December 31, 2011.

Everglades National Park

Water-level gage P37 is located in the Everglades National Park (fig. 3) and has a 59-year period of record from 1953 to 2011 (table 1) with a mean water level of 1.28 ft (table 7). For the period of record, water levels were lowest during period 2 (1955–1957) with a mean of 0.70 ft, and highest during period 3 (1957–1961) with a mean of 1.57 ft (fig. 10; table 7). The largest increasing shift in water levels between subsequent periods occurred between periods 2 and 3 (1955–1957 and 1957–1961, respectively) with a value of 0.87 ft based on the mean (table 7). The largest decreasing shift in water levels between subsequent periods occurred between periods 1 and 2 (1953–1955 and 1955–1957, respectively) with a value of –0.73 ft based on the mean (table 7).

Analysis of Concurrent Period

The cumulative Z-score curves and cumulative frequency distribution curves for the concurrent period of record, October 12, 1978, to December 31, 2011, associated with the water-level gages listed in table 1 are presented in this section. Using a concurrent period of record between the six gages allows for comparison of water levels in the WCAs and Everglades National Park. The period of record for Site 99 (fig. 3) extends from 1991 to 2011 (table 1), which is shorter than the concurrent period of analysis. Therefore, the only analysis at this site was for the period of record as presented previously in this report (fig. 8; table 4). The period of record (January 1, 1978, to December 31, 2011) for water-level gage 3ANE (fig. 3; table 1) is similar to the concurrent period of analysis, October 12, 1978, to December 31, 2011. Therefore, it was decided to only analyze the concurrent period of record as presented previously in this report (fig. 9; table 5). Plots of the cumulative Z-score and daily water-level and cumulative water-level frequency curves for Site 7, Site 17, Site 64, and station P37 are shown in figures 11–14, respectively. The means, standard deviations, 50th percentiles, and averages of the 5th to 95th percentiles associated with the cumulative frequency distribution curves for Site 7, Site 17, station 3ANE, Site 64, and station P37 are listed in tables 2, 3, 5, 6, and 7, respectively, along with the change in the values of the mean, 50th percentile, and average of the 5th to 95th percentiles from the previous period.

Table 6. Selected statistics for the cumulative water-level frequency distribution curves for selected time periods at Site 64 in Water Conservation Area 3A in the Florida Everglades.

[NGVD 29, National Geodetic Vertical Datum of 1929]

Period	Start date	End date	Number of observations	Standard deviation, in feet	Mean, in feet NGVD 29	50th Percentile water level, in feet NGVD 29	Average 5th–95th percentile water level, in feet NGVD 29	Change from previous period		
								Mean, in feet	50th Percentile water level, in feet	Average 5th–95th percentile water level, in feet
						Period of Record—April 6, 1962, to December 31, 2011				
1	April 6, 1962	May 1, 1966	1,276	0.78	8.63	8.67	8.68			
2	May 1, 1966	January 1, 1971	1,663	0.75	9.92	9.99	9.95	1.29	1.32	1.28
3	January 1, 1971	July 1, 1977	2,289	0.96	8.77	8.74	8.81	−1.15	−1.25	−1.14
4	July 1, 1977	December 1, 1988	4,172	0.73	9.68	9.80	9.72	0.91	1.06	0.91
5	December 1, 1988	January 1, 1992	1,127	0.80	8.79	8.73	8.78	−0.89	−1.07	−0.94
6	January 1, 1992	February 1, 2000	2,901	0.85	10.49	10.49	10.46	1.70	1.76	1.69
7	February 1, 2000	August 1, 2001	546	0.49	9.52	9.42	9.52	−0.97	−1.08	−0.95
8	August 1, 2001	January 1, 2006	1,598	0.79	10.44	10.44	10.45	0.92	1.03	0.93
9	January 1, 2006	December 31, 2011	2,163	0.83	9.89	9.91	9.90	−0.55	−0.53	−0.55
Record	April 6, 1962	December 31, 2011	17,727	1.03	9.68	9.74	9.69			
			Concurrent Period—October 12, 1978, to December 31, 2011							
1	October 12, 1978	December 1, 1980	782	0.39	9.90	9.87	9.91			
2	December 1, 1980	June 1, 1982	548	0.78	8.99	8.98	8.99	−0.91	−0.89	−0.92
3	June 1, 1982	November 1, 1988	2,346	0.75	9.78	9.94	9.82	0.79	0.96	0.83
4	November 1, 1988	July 1, 1991	973	0.58	8.56	8.61	8.56	−1.22	−1.33	−1.26
5	July 1, 1991	August 1, 1994	1,128	0.56	10.13	10.21	10.15	1.57	1.60	1.60
6	August 1, 1994	January 1, 1996	500	0.94	11.34	11.50	11.36	1.21	1.29	1.20
7	January 1, 1996	February 1, 2000	1,459	0.75	10.44	10.57	10.41	−0.90	−0.93	−0.95
8	February 1, 2000	August 1, 2001	546	0.49	9.52	9.42	9.52	−0.92	−1.16	−0.89
9	August 1, 2001	March 1, 2006	1,657	0.78	10.44	10.43	10.45	0.92	1.02	0.93
10	March 1, 2006	December 31, 2011	2,104	0.84	9.88	9.88	9.88	−0.56	−0.56	−0.56
Record	October 12, 1978	December 31, 2011	12,034	0.94	9.93	9.98	9.93			

Table 7.   Selected statistics for the cumulative water-level frequency distribution curves for selected time periods at station P37 in Water Conservation Area 3A in the Florida Everglades.

[NGVD 29, National Geodetic Vertical Datum of 1929]

Period	Start date	End date	Number of observations	Standard deviation, in feet	Mean, in feet NGVD 29	50th Percentile water level, in feet NGVD 29	Average 5th–95th percentile water level, in feet NGVD 29	Change from previous period		
								Mean, in feet	50th Percentile water level, in feet	Average 5th–95th percentile water level, in feet
Period of Record—January 15, 1953, to December 31, 2011										
1	January 15, 1953	January 1, 1955	717	0.51	1.43	1.48	1.48			
2	January 1, 1955	June 1, 1957	883	0.77	0.70	0.87	0.74	−0.73	−0.61	−0.74
3	June 1, 1957	January 1, 1961	1,311	0.42	1.57	1.55	1.58	0.87	0.68	0.84
4	January 1, 1961	January 1, 1970	3,288	0.72	1.12	1.23	1.17	−0.45	−0.32	−0.40
5	January 1, 1970	January 1, 1977	2,557	0.77	0.96	1.17	1.03	−0.16	−0.06	−0.14
6	January 1, 1977	January 1, 1989	4,250	0.46	1.34	1.40	1.36	0.38	0.23	0.33
7	January 1, 1989	January 1, 1992	1,096	0.80	0.84	1.05	0.87	−0.50	−0.35	−0.49
8	January 1, 1992	January 1, 2004	4,384	0.49	1.55	1.60	1.57	0.71	0.55	0.70
9	January 1, 2004	December 31, 2011	2,922	0.64	1.39	1.47	1.43	−0.16	−0.13	−0.14
Record	January 15, 1953	December 31, 2011	21,400	0.66	1.28	1.38	1.32			
Concurrent Period—October 12, 1978, to December 31, 2011										
1	October 12, 1978	December 1, 1980	782	0.42	1.37	1.46	1.40			
2	December 1, 1980	June 1, 1982	516	0.48	1.20	1.23	1.20	−0.17	−0.23	−0.20
3	June 1, 1982	November 1, 1988	2,244	0.48	1.38	1.45	1.40	0.18	0.22	0.19
4	November 1, 1988	July 1, 1991	973	0.76	0.71	0.97	0.75	−0.67	−0.48	−0.64
5	July 1, 1991	August 1, 1994	1,128	0.41	1.44	1.48	1.46	0.73	0.51	0.71
6	August 1, 1994	January 1, 1996	519	0.37	1.88	1.90	1.88	0.44	0.42	0.42
7	January 1, 1996	February 1, 2000	1,493	0.46	1.61	1.67	1.63	−0.27	−0.23	−0.25
8	February 1, 2000	August 1, 2001	548	0.55	1.20	1.27	1.21	−0.41	−0.40	−0.42
9	August 1, 2001	March 1, 2006	1,674	0.64	1.47	1.57	1.51	0.27	0.30	0.30
10	March 1, 2006	December 31, 2011	2,132	0.59	1.43	1.51	1.47	−0.04	−0.06	−0.04
Record	October 12, 1978	December 31, 2011	12,000	0.59	1.39	1.47	1.42			

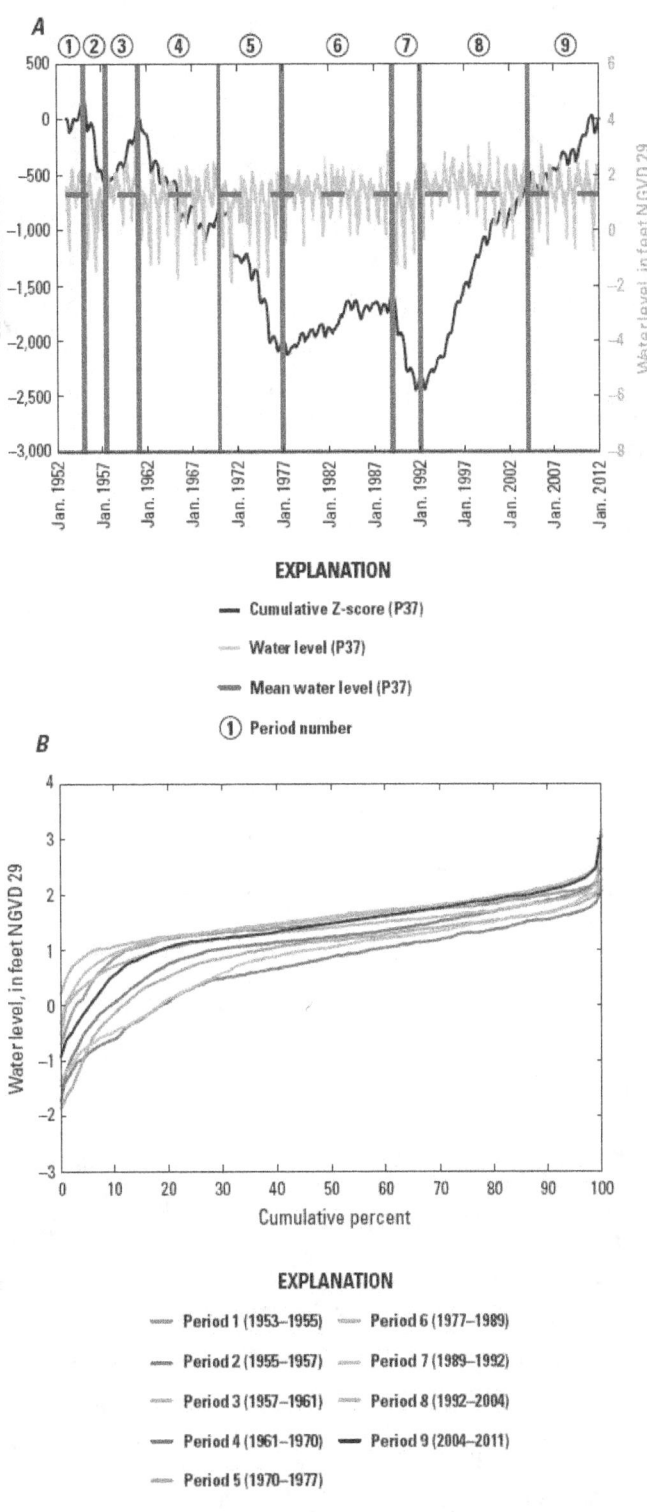

Figure 10. (*A*) Cumulative Z-score curve and daily water-level data and (*B*) cumulative water-level frequency distribution curves for station P37 in the Everglades National Park for the period January 15, 1953, to December 31, 2011.

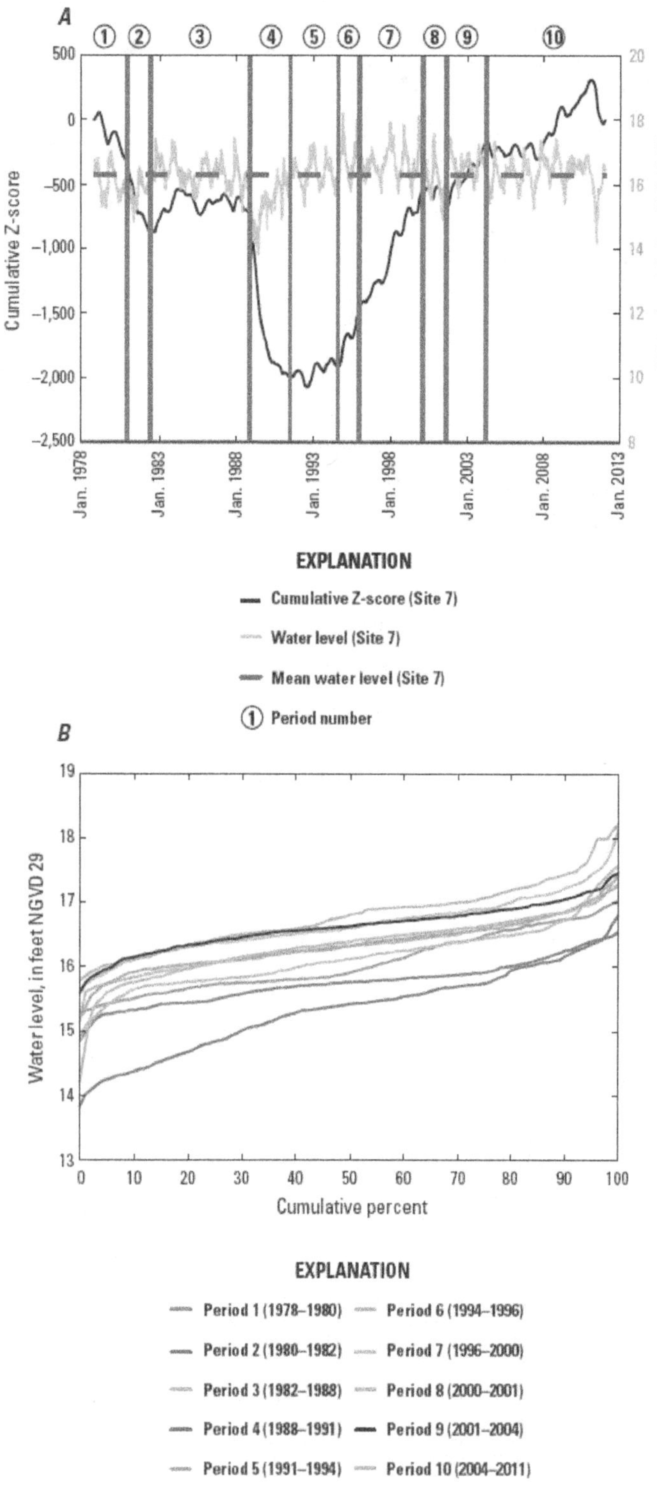

Figure 11. (*A*) Cumulative Z-score curve and daily water-level data and (*B*) cumulative water-level frequency distribution curves for Site 7 in Water Conservation Area 1 for the period October 12, 1978, to December 31, 2011.

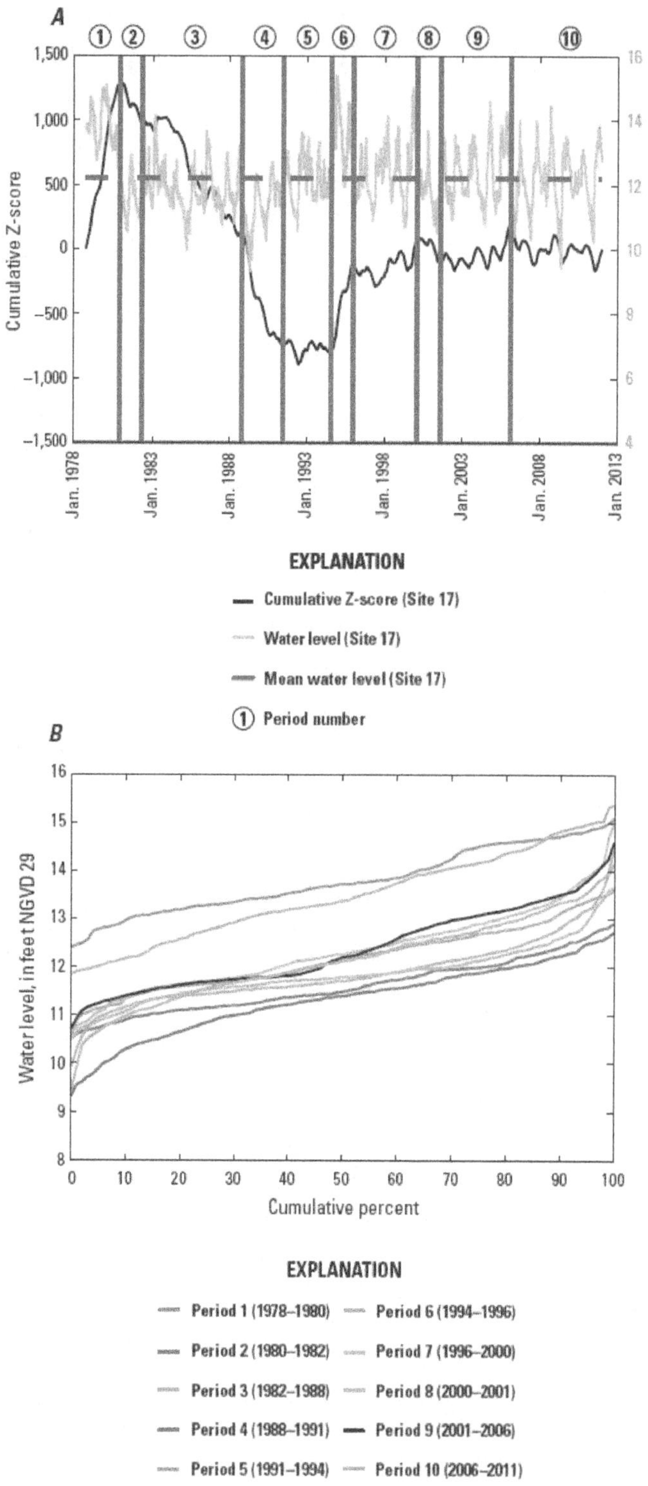

Figure 12. (*A*) Cumulative Z-score curve and daily water level data and (*B*) cumulative water level frequency distribution curves for Site 17 in Water Conservation Area 2A for the period October 12, 1978 to December 31, 2011.

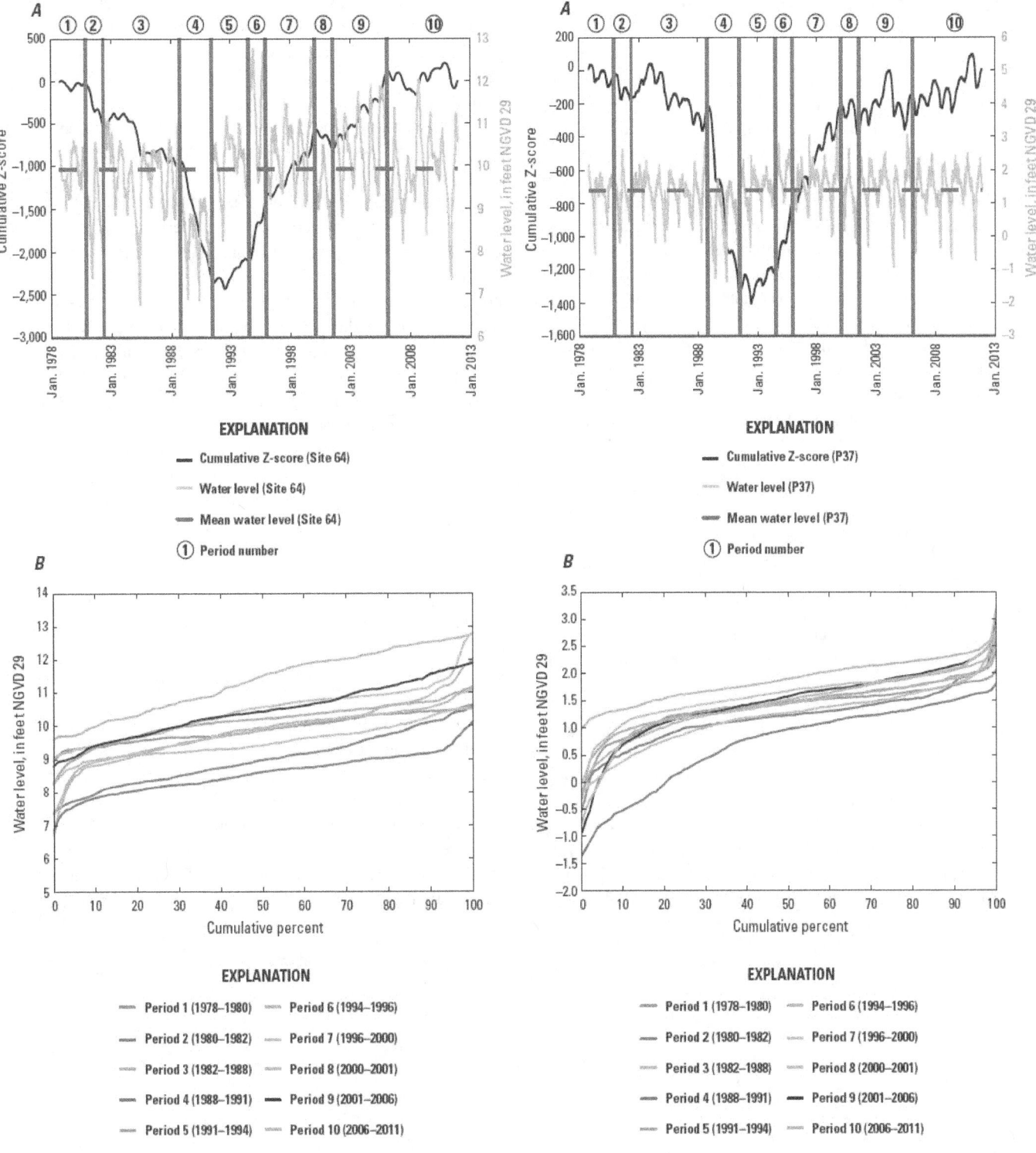

Figure 13 (*A*) Cumulative Z-score curve and daily water-level data and (*B*) cumulative water-level frequency distribution curves for Site 64 in Water Conservation Area 3A for the period October 12, 1978, to December 31, 2011.

Figure 14. (*A*) Cumulative Z-score curve and daily water-level data and (*B*) cumulative water-level frequency distribution curves for station P37 in Water Conservation Area 3A for the period October 12, 1978, to December 31, 2011.

Comparison of Time Series Water-Level Data Among Sites

Figure 15A shows the cumulative Z-score curves for the six water-level gages for the concurrent period of analysis along with the break points used in the analyses (vertical red lines). As can be seen, the cumulative Z-score curves have similar shape and break points. While the change in the slope may be less pronounced in some curves compared to others, the general response for all the curves is similar. Because the six water-level gages are part of an interconnected system within the Everglades, it is reasonable to expect similar responses among the gages. The time-series water-level data for all gages for the concurrent period of analysis are shown in figure 15B along with the same break points from figure 15A. The break points provide a visual aid to help identify changes within the water-level behavior, in particular some of the more subtle changes. While each set of gage data has unique features, the response patterns are similar. It is interesting to note that the response patterns of the water level at the northernmost gage, Site 7 in WCA-1, and the southernmost gage, station P37 in the Everglades National Park, although separated by approximately 90 miles, are similar. Again, this pattern highlights the interconnectedness of the Everglades system.

To better compare the general patterns between the water-level gages during the concurrent period of analysis, the average 5th to 95th percentile water levels based on the 10 periods (periods between break points) associated with the cumulative frequency distribution curves (tables 2–7) were plotted in several ways. Figure 16 shows the values for the average 5th to 95th percentile water levels at five of the gages with respect to the 10 periods. (Note: The analysis at Site 99 was not included in the following comparisons because the period of record [1991–2011] did not encompass the concurrent period.) The general patterns between the gages are similar, with the lowest and highest values at each gage occurring in periods 4 and 6, respectively. An exception to this occurs at Site 17 where the largest water level occurs in period 1.

While the general shape for each curve is similar, there is a larger range in water-level fluctuation at Site 17, station 3ANE, and Site 64 located in WCAs 2 and 3 (fig. 3), than at Site 7 and station P37 located in WCA-1 and the Everglades National Park (fig. 3), respectively.

To more readily compare the trends of the data presented in figure 16, it is possible to standardize the average 5th to 95th percentile water levels to provide a common comparison scale. In figure 17, the data were standardized by taking the difference between the average 5th to 95th percentile water level for each of the 10 periods of analysis and that of the full concurrent period (1978–2011). These standardized data show the relative difference in water level for the 10 periods with respect to the mean for the full concurrent period (1978–2011). The common scale in figure 17 highlights the patterns observed in figure 16 including the similarity in curve patterns for all the gages, the occurrence of the low and high extremes in periods 4 and 6, respectively, and the larger variability at Site 17, station 3ANE, and Site 64. It also is possible to standardize the data in figure 16 using the Z-score (eqs. 1–3). The individual Z-score at a given gage and period is computed by taking the average 5th to 95th percentile water level for a given period, subtracting the mean of the average 5th to 95th percentile water level for the 10 periods, and dividing by the standard deviation of the average 5th to 95th percentile water level for the 10 periods. The Z-score values represent the number of standard deviations that the average 5th to 95th percentile water level for a given period is above or below the mean of the average 5th to 95th percentile water level for the 10 periods. (Note: The individual Z-score described above should not be confused with the cumulative Z-score used in the break-point analysis.) Figure 18 shows the Z-scores at each gage for the average 5th to 95th percentile water levels for the 10 periods and confirms the general patterns observed in figures 16 and 17 with the exception that the larger variabilities at Site 17, station 3ANE, and Site 64 are less pronounced.

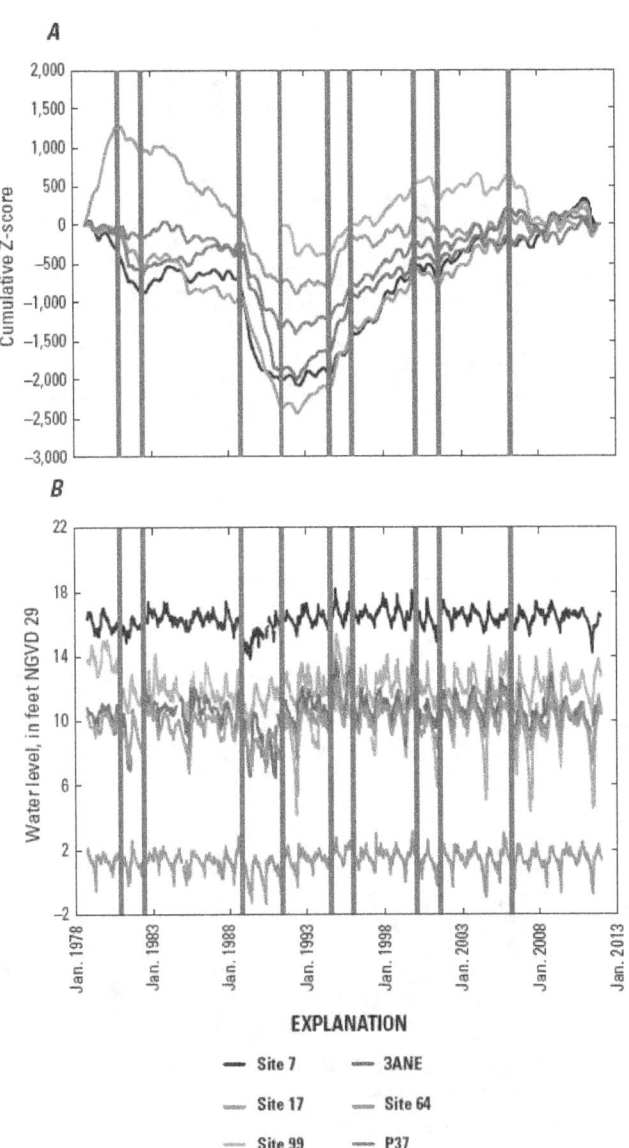

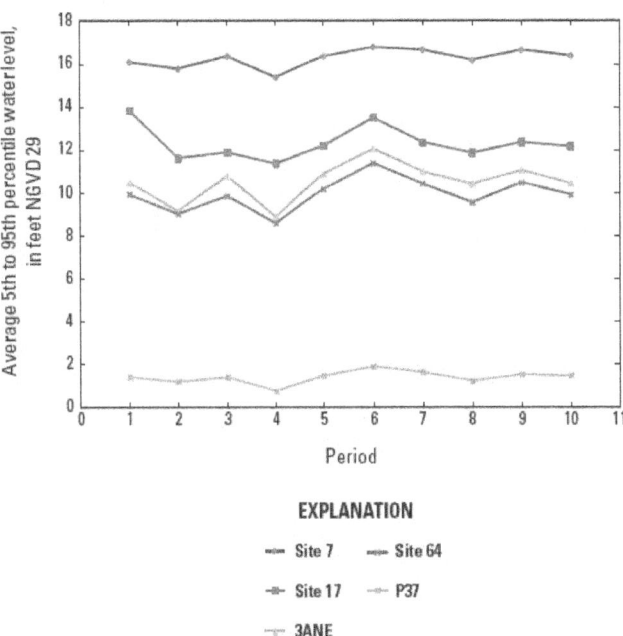

Figure 16. Relation of the average 5th to 95th percentile water levels with respect to the 10 periods of analysis for selected gages in the Florida Everglades for the period October 12, 1978, to December 31, 2011.

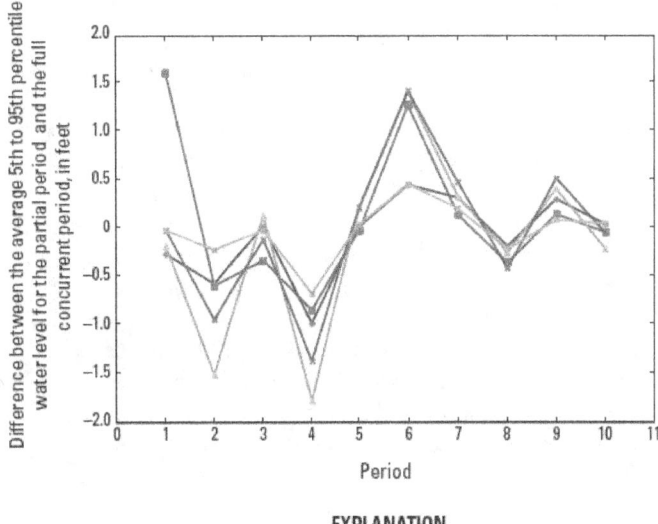

Figure 15. (*A*) Cumulative Z-score curves and (*B*) water-level data for selected water-level gages in the Florida Everglades for the period October 12, 1978, to December 31, 2011.

Figure 17. Relation of the difference between the average 5th to 95th percentile water level for the 10 periods of analysis and that of the full concurrent period (1978–2011) for selected gages in the Florida Everglades.

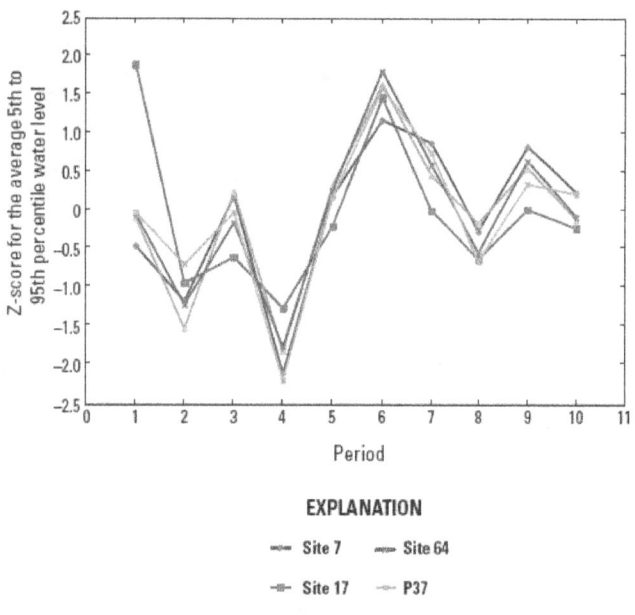

EXPLANATION

—•— Site 7   —•— Site 64

—■— Site 17   —○— P37

—•— 3ANE

Figure 18. Relation of the Z-score for the average 5th to 95th percentile water levels with respect to the 10 periods of analysis for selected gages in the Florida Everglades.

Figures 19, 20, and 21 respectively show the ranges of the water-level fluctuations, the largest water-level increases between consecutive periods, and the largest water-level decreases between consecutive periods for each gage. These figures show the larger variability in water-level fluctuations at Site 17, station 3ANE, and Site 64. Figures 20 and 21 indicate that the largest increases and decreases in water level between consecutive periods occur during the same consecutive periods (from period 4 to 5 and from period 3 to 4, respectively) at all gages except Site 17, highlighting the similarity in response patterns at each gage. The largest increase in water level between consecutive periods at Site 17 occurs from periods 5 to 6, which is close chronologically to the consecutive periods, from period 4 to 5, in which the other gages display the largest increase. The largest decrease in water level between consecutive periods at Site 17 occurs from period 1 to 2 and is caused by the unusually high water levels at the beginning of period 1 (fig. 12A).

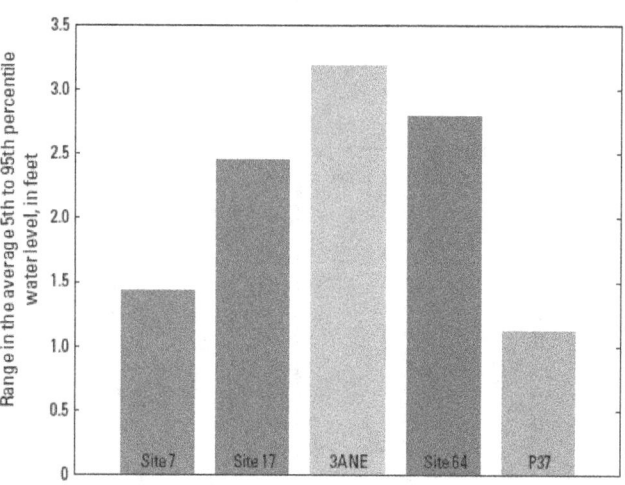

Figure 19. Range of water-level fluctuation based on the average 5th to 95th percentile water levels for the 10 periods of analysis at selected gages in the Florida Everglades.

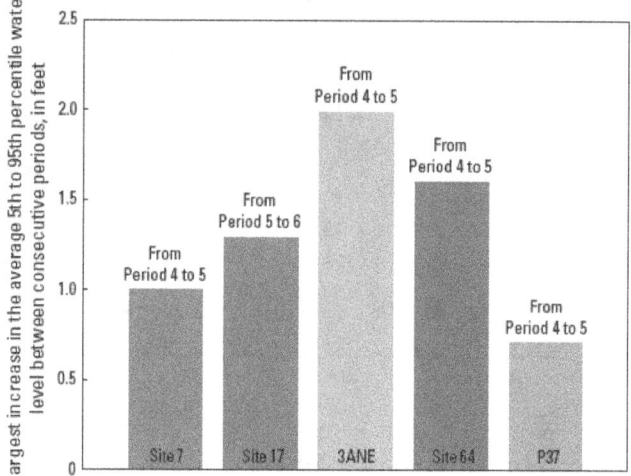

Figure 20. Largest increase in water level between consecutive periods based on the average 5th to 95th percentile water levels for the 10 periods of analysis at selected gages in the Florida Everglades.

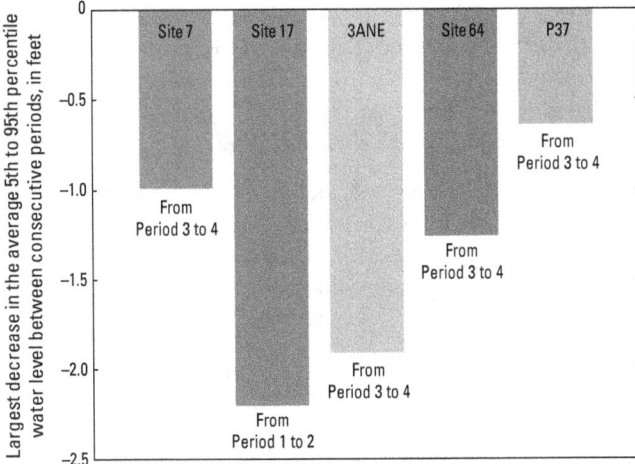

Figure 21. Largest decrease in water level between consecutive periods based on the average 5th to 95th percentile water levels for the 10 periods of analysis at selected gages in the Florida Everglades.

Summary

The U.S. Geological Survey, through its Greater Everglades Priority Ecosystem Science and National Water-Quality Assessment Programs, has been involved in data collection, data management, and field investigations within the Florida Everglades with a primary objective of providing scientific information to assist resource managers in the Everglades restoration efforts. A primary task of the current investigation was to develop a simple method to identify changes in historical hydrologic behavior within the Everglades that could be used by researchers to identify responses of ecological communities to those changes. Such information could in turn be used by resource managers to develop appropriate water-management practices within the Everglades to promote the restoration and health of the Everglades ecosystem. The identification of historical hydrologic behavior within the Everglades was accomplished by analyzing historical time-series water-level data from selected gages in the Everglades using (1) break-point analysis of cumulative Z-scores to identify changes in hydrologic behavior and (2) cumulative water-level frequency distribution curves to evaluate the magnitude of those changes. This analytical technique was applied to six long-term water-level gages in the Florida Everglades located near the U.S. Geological Survey Aquatic Cycling of Mercury in the Everglades Project sampling sites so that results from the investigation could be used to support the research efforts in those areas. The cumulative Z-score analysis was applied for the period of record at each individual gage as well as for the concurrent period of October 12, 1978, to December 31, 2011. The break-point analysis for the concurrent period of record (1978–2011) identified 10 common periods of changes in hydrologic behavior at the selected gages. The water-level responses at each gage for the 10 periods displayed similarity in fluctuation patterns, highlighting the interconnectedness of the Florida Everglades hydrologic system. While the patterns were similar, the analysis also showed that larger fluctuations in water levels occur in Water Conservation Areas 2 and 3 in contrast to those in Water Conservation Area 1 and the Everglades National Park. Results from the analysis indicate that the cumulative Z-score curve in conjunction with cumulative water-level frequency distribution curves can be a useful tool in identifying and quantifying changes in historical hydrologic behavior within the Everglades. In addition to the analysis, a spreadsheet application, the Z-scores for Everglades Breakpoint Analysis (ZEBRA), was developed to assist in applying these techniques to time-series water-level data at other gages within the Everglades.

Selected References

Briceño, H.O., Boyer, J.N., and Harlem, P.W., 2010, Proposed methodology for the assessment of numeric nutrient criteria for South Florida estuaries and coastal waters, Report to the National Park Service, Everglades National Park, Cooperative Agreement Number: H5000-06-0104, 44 p.

Buishand, T.A., 1982, Some methods for testing the homogeneity of rainfall records: Journal of Hydrology, v. 58, no. 1–2, p. 11–27.

Davis, J.H., Jr., 1943, Vegetation map of Southern Florida: Florida Geological Survey, Bulletin 25, figure 71, 1 sheet, 1:400,000 scale.

Florida Department of Environmental Protection, 2011, Mercury in aquatic ecosystems in Florida, accessed June 25, 2012, at *http://www.dep.state.fl.us/water/sas/mercury/index.htm.*

Iman, R.L., and Conover, W.J., 1983, A modern approach to statistics: John Wiley and Sons, Inc., 497 p.

Krabbenhoft, D.P., Gilmour, C.C., Orem, W.H., Aiken, G.R., Kendall, Carol, Olsen, M.L., and DeWild, John, 2000, Aquatic Cycling of Mercury in the Everglades (ACME) Project—Synopis of Phase I Studies and Plans for Phase II Studies, *in* Eggleston, J.R., Embry, T.L., Mooney, R.H., Wedderburn, Leslie, Goodwin, C.R., Henkel, H.S., Pegram, K.M.H., and Enright, T.J., 2001, Presentations made at the Greater Everglades Ecosystem Restoration (GEER) Conference, December 11–15, 2000, Naples, Florida: U.S. Geological Survey Open-File Report 00-449, p. 62–63.

McPherson, B.F., Higer, A.L., Gerould, S., and Kantrowitz, I.H., 1995, South Florida Ecosystem Program of the U.S. Geological Survey: U.S. Geological Survey Fact Sheet FS-134-95, accessed June 19, 2012, at *http://sofia.usgs.gov/publications/fs/134-95/index.html.*

Richardson, J.R., Bryant, W.L., Kitchens, W.M., Mattson, J.E., and Pope, K.R., 1990, An evaluation of the refuge habitats and relationships to water quality, quantity, and hydroperiods—A synthesis report: Gainesville, Fla., Florida Cooperative Fish and Wildlife Research Unit, University of Florida.

Rodionov, S.N., 2005, A brief overview of the regime shift detection methods, *in* Velikova, V., and Chipev, N., eds., Large-scale disturbances (regime shifts) and recovery in aquatic ecosystems—Challenges for management toward sustainability: Varna, Bulgaria, June 14–16, 2005, UNESCO-ROSTE/BAS Workshop on Regime Shifts, p. 17–24.

South Florida Water Management District, 2011, DBHYDRO Browser user documentation, accessed July 9, 2012, at *http://www.sfwmd.gov/portal/page/portal/xweb%20environmental%20monitoring/dbhydro%20application.*

Telis, P.A., 2006, The Everglades Depth Estimation Network (EDEN) for support of ecological and biological assessments: U.S. Geological Survey Fact Sheet 2006-3087, 4 p.

U.S. Fish and Wildlife Service, 2000, Arthur R. Marshall Loxahatchee National Wildlife Refuge Comprehensive Conservation Plan, accessed September 13, 2010, at *http://loxahatchee.fws.gov.*

Appendix. Overview of the Z-Scores for Everglades Breakpoint Analysis Application

Figures

Screen captures showing—

1-1.   ZEBRA title sheet...31
1-2.   ZEBRA worksheet showing water-level data for selected gages...............................33
1-3.   ZEBRA worksheet showing computation tables or the cumulative Z-score
        and cumulative water-level frequency distribution curves.......................................34
1-4.   ZEBRA worksheet for selecting break points for the cumulative Z-score
        curve and plots of the cumulative water-level frequency distribution curves
        for the periods between the selected break points..35
1-5.   ZEBRA worksheet for tabulation of basic statistics for each cumulative
        water-level frequency distribution curve...36

Table

1–1.   Description of worksheets and applications included in ZEBRA.......................................32

Appendix. Overview of the Z-Scores for Everglades Breakpoint Analysis Application

A break-point analysis using the cumulative Z-score and cumulative frequency distribution curves, as briefly described in the body of this report, is a simple technique to apply to a given dataset. However, the application can become challenging for large datasets, such as daily average water-level data associated with gages in the Everglades that often have long periods of record extending over decades. To minimize this difficulty, a spreadsheet application called the Z-scores for Everglades Breakpoint Analysis (ZEBRA) (fig. 1–1), was developed to assist in applying the analytical techniques. ZEBRA provides a means to (1) store selected water-level data, (2) compute the cumulative Z-score for the selected data, (3) plot the selected cumulative Z-score curve so that break points can be visually identified, and (4) manually enter break-point data that will be used to automatically generate the cumulative water-level frequency distribution curves. The worksheets that compose ZEBRA are listed in table 1–1. A brief description of ZEBRA follows.

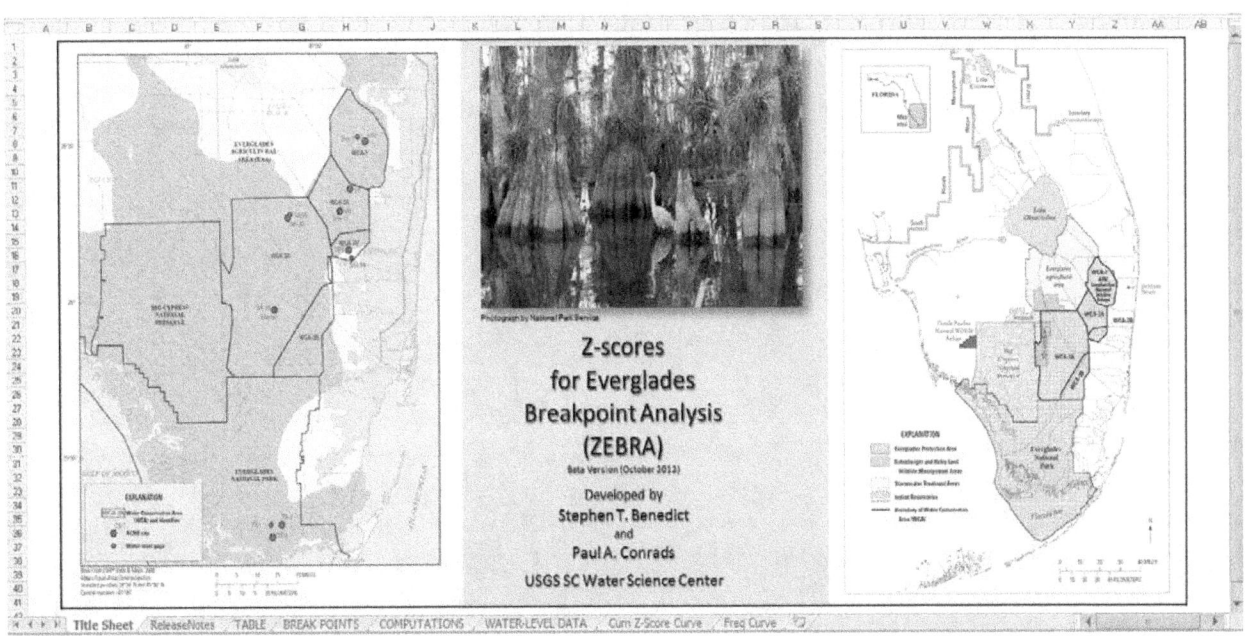

Figure 1-1.   Screen capture of ZEBRA title sheet.

Table 1–1.   Description of worksheets and applications included in ZEBRA.

[ZEBRA, Z-scores for Everglades Breakpoint Analysis]

Worksheet Name	Description
Title Sheet	Title sheet for ZEBRA.
ReleaseNotes	Selected information associated with ZEBRA and a description of each worksheet.
TABLE	Basic statistics for each cumulative water-level frequency distribution curve are automatically calculated and tabulated.
BREAK POINTS	Graphs displaying the water-level, cumulative Z-score curve, and the cumulative water-level frequency distribution curves for the gage of interest. The user can enter selected break points into the break-point table, and the cumulative water-level frequency distribution curves will be automatically computed and plotted. (Note: Dropdown menus allow the user to select the gage of interest for display.)
COMPUTATIONS	Computations for the cumulative Z-score curve and the cumulative water-level frequency distribution curves are made on this sheet. Data from this worksheet are used in the spreadsheet graphs.
WATER-LEVEL DATA	Tabulation of water-level data at selected gages in the Florida Everglades.
Cum Z-Score Curve	Full graph of cumulative Z-score curve, water-level data, and break points for the selected gage.
Freq Curve	Full graph of cumulative water-level frequency distribution curves for the selected gage.

Water-Level Data and Computation of Cumulative Z-Scores and Frequency Distribution Curves

The DBHYDRO database (South Florida Water Management District: *http://www.sfwmd.gov/portal/page/portal/xweb%20environmental%20monitoring/dbhydro%20application*, accessed July 9, 2012) is the hydrometeorologic, water-quality, and hydrogeologic data retrieval system for the South Florida Water Management District. The database is maintained through a cooperative effort of various agencies including the U.S. Geological Survey, Everglades National Park, the U.S. Army Corps of Engineers, Lake Worth Drainage District, and the U.S. Department of Agriculture and includes more than 30,000 station-years of data, collected at more than 6,000 stations (South Florida Water Management District, 2011). Water-level data for gages in the Florida Everglades can be queried and retrieved through the DBHYDRO Browser

located at the previously mentioned Web page. The data can be downloaded in a spreadsheet format allowing the transfer of the data into ZEBRA through a simple "copy and paste" command. The water-level data at a given gage in DBHYDRO is often broken into several records that must be manually combined in order to obtain a complete record. In some cases, there may be overlap and slight differences between the broken records, and judgment must be applied to decide which data to use in compiling the complete record. Once a complete water-level data record is compiled for a gage of interest, the data can be copied into ZEBRA. Figure 1–2 shows a screen capture of the ZEBRA worksheet "WATER-LEVEL DATA," which contains the water-level data for the gages analyzed in this report. Dates corresponding with the water-level data are in the first column of the worksheet, and the water-level data are entered to correspond with those dates. The header cells above the water-level data provide information on the gage location, the period of record, and basic statistics associated with the dataset.

	A	B	C	D	E	F	G	H
2		**Daily Water-Level Data for Selected Gages in the Florida Everglades**						
4		Compiled July 2012						
5		NOTE: empty cells are missing data or unprocessed data at the time the data was obtained.						
7	Area	WCA 1	WCA 2A	WCA 2B	WCA 3A	WCA 3A	ENP
8	Station	1-7	Site 17	28-99	3A-NE	Site 64	P37
9	Data Type	STG	STG	STG	STG	STG	STG
10	Statistic	MEAN	MEAN	MEAN	MEAN	MEAN	MEAN
11	Start Date	1-Jan-1954	10-Jun-1952	12-Jul-1991	1-Jan-1978	6-Apr-1962	15-Jan-1953
12	End Date	31-Dec-2011	31-Dec-2011	31-Dec-2011	31-Dec-2011	31-Dec-2011	31-Dec-2011
13	UTM Easting Zone 17N (meters NAD83)	565061.9	558814	863759.68	539459.1	533110	531371.1
14	UTM Northing Zone 17N (meters NAD83)	2933415.4	2907573.8	656776.90	2906638.9	2873028.9	2796463.3
15	Latitude (DMS) NAD83	263134.254	261712	260821.00	261644	255832	251703
16	Longitude (DMS) NAD83	802019.17	802439	802202	803617	804009	804118
17	Total Days in Period of Record	21184	21754	7478	12418	18167	21535
18	Missing Days	774	536	139	669	440	135
19	COUNT	20410	21218	7339	11749	17727	21400
20	MIN	13.83	9.33	4.16	6.30	5.95	-1.87
21	MAX	18.21	15.64	11.89	13.81	12.79	3.17
22	MEDIAN	16.15	12.29	10.19	10.67	9.74	1.38
23	AVERAGE	16.12	12.41	9.84	10.59	9.68	1.28
24	STDEVP	0.61	1.06	1.28	1.05	1.03	0.66
25	Daily Date	Water Level (feet - NGVD29)	Water Level (feet - NGVD29)	Water Level (feet - NGVD29)	Water Level (feet - NGVD29)	Water Level (feet - NGVD29)	Water Level (feet - NGVD29)
27	11-Jun-1952		10.23				
28	12-Jun-1952		10.18				
29	13-Jun-1952		10.13				
30	14-Jun-1952		10.08				
31	15-Jun-1952		10.02				
32	16-Jun-1952		9.97				

Title Sheet / ReleaseNotes / TABLE / BREAK POINTS / COMPUTATIONS / WATER-LEVEL DATA / Cum Z-Score Curve / Freq Curve

Figure 1-2. Screen capture of ZEBRA worksheet showing water-level data for selected gages.

Figure 1–3 shows a screen capture of the ZEBRA worksheet "COMPUTATIONS," which computes the cumulative Z-score and cumulative water-level frequency distribution curves for the gage of interest. The header cells above the frequency distribution curves provide information about the period of analysis between break points and basic statistics associated with each of the periods. The gage of interest can be selected from the dropdown menu near the upper left corner of the worksheet, and the gage data and user-defined break points for the selected gage will be automatically retrieved from the "WATER-LEVEL DATA" and "BREAK POINTS" worksheets, respectively. The cumulative Z-score and cumulative water-level frequency distribution curves are then automatically computed. Data contained in the COMPUTATIONS worksheet are used to produce the graphs found in ZEBRA.

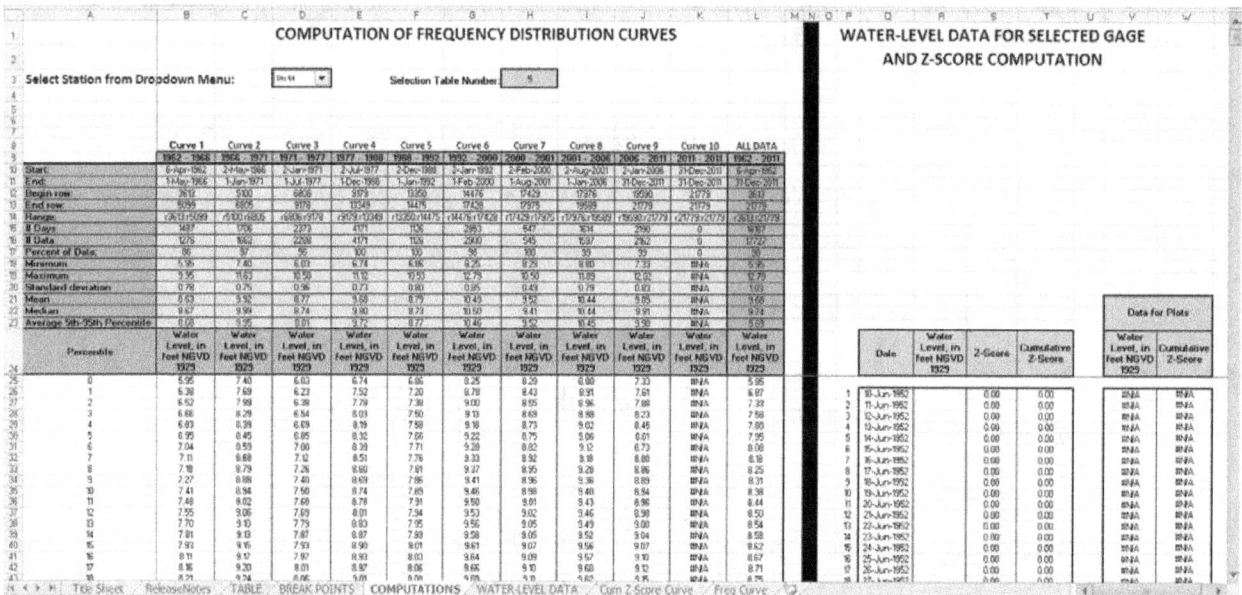

Figure 1-3.   Screen capture of ZEBRA worksheet showing computation tables for the cumulative Z-score and cumulative water-level frequency distribution curves.

Selection of Break Points for the Cumulative Z-Score Curve

Figure 1–4 shows a screen capture of the ZEBRA worksheet "BREAK POINTS." This worksheet allows the user to visually identify and manually enter break points for a given cumulative Z-score curve that in turn are used to develop the cumulative water-level frequency distribution curves for the gage of interest. The gage of interest can be selected from the dropdown menu near the upper left corner of the worksheet. (Note: The dropdown menu on this worksheet is linked to the dropdown menu on the "COMPUTATIONS" worksheet.) The water-level data and cumulative Z-score curves for the selected gage are automatically plotted on the graph

at the bottom right of this worksheet (fig. 1–4), allowing the user to visually identify break points where the slope of the cumulative Z-score curve changes. The dates associated with these break points can then be entered into the Break-Point Table located near the top of the worksheet. The column in the Break-Point Table associated with the selected gage is highlighted in green indicating where the break-point dates should be entered. ZEBRA can accommodate a maximum of nine break points. These break points are automatically plotted as red vertical lines on the cumulative Z-score curve. The cumulative water-level frequency distribution curves for the periods between the selected break points are automatically computed on the "COMPUTATIONS" worksheet and plotted on the graph located on the bottom left of the "BREAK POINTS" worksheet (fig. 1–4).

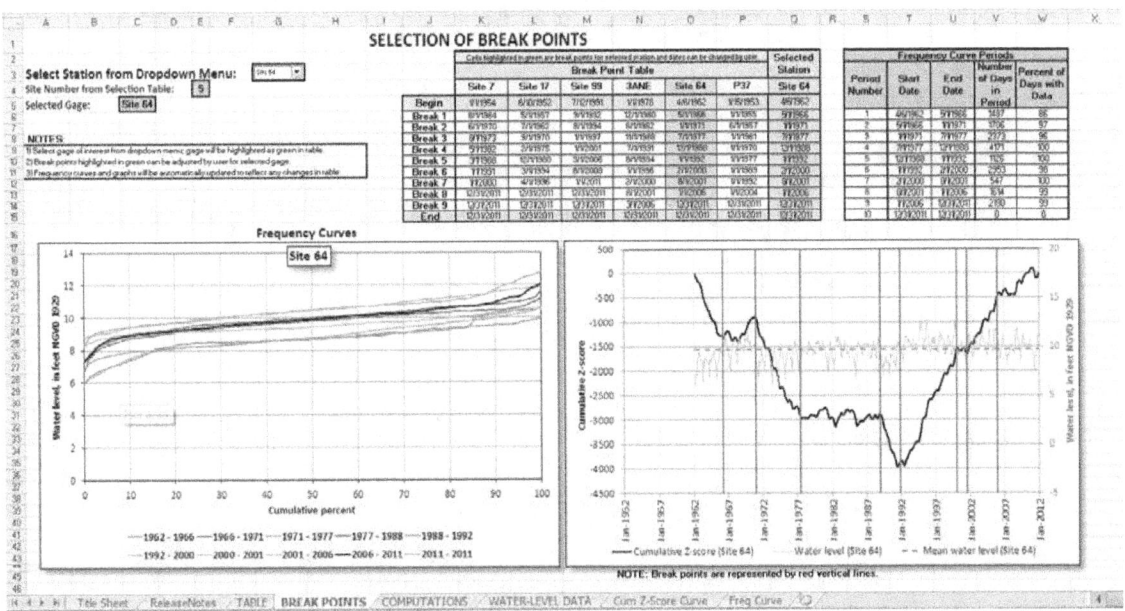

Figure 1-4. Screen capture showing ZEBRA worksheet for selecting break points for the cumulative Z-score curve and plots of the cumulative water-level frequency distribution curves for the periods between the selected break points.

Basic statistics for each cumulative water-level frequency distribution curve are automatically calculated and tabulated on the "TABLE" worksheet (fig. 1–5). Additionally, the start and end dates for the periods between the selected break points along with the number of days within the period and the percentage of available data in that period are tabulated in the Frequency Curve Periods table in the upper right corner of the "BREAK POINTS" worksheet (fig. 1–4). A larger plot of the two graphs shown at the bottom of the "BREAK POINTS" worksheet can be viewed on the worksheets labeled "Cum Z-Score Curve" and "Freq Curve."

Using ZEBRA with Other Data

It is possible to use ZEBRA to analyze water-level data at other gages in the Everglades; however, caution must be used to not exceed the cell ranges built into the spreadsheet algorithms. To analyze data at another gage, the existing data in the spreadsheet can be overwritten. The cell ranges used to store the existing data should not be exceeded by the new data, however, and the new data must be entered in the appropriate cell to correspond with the dates in the first column of the "WATER-LEVEL DATA" worksheet. Additionally, the identification data in the column headers of the "WATER-LEVEL DATA" worksheet must be changed to reflect the new gage.

SELECTED STATISTICS FOR FREQUENCY DISTRIBUTION CURVES

Site: Site 64

Period	Start Date	End Date	Number of observations	Standard Deviation	Mean, in feet NGVD 1929	50th Percentile water level, in feet NGVD 1929	Average 5th-95th Percentile water level, in feet NGVD 1929	Change from previous period		
								Mean, in feet NGVD 1929	50th Percentile water level, in feet NGVD 1929	Average 5th-95th Percentile water level, in feet NGVD 1929
1	April 6, 1962	May 1, 1966	1276	0.78	8.63	8.67	8.68			
2	May 2, 1966	January 1, 1971	1662	0.75	9.92	9.99	9.95	1.29	1.32	1.28
3	January 2, 1971	July 1, 1977	2288	0.96	8.77	8.74	8.81	-1.15	-1.25	-1.15
4	July 2, 1977	December 1, 1988	4171	0.73	9.68	9.80	9.72	0.91	1.06	0.91
5	December 2, 1988	January 1, 1992	1126	0.80	8.79	8.73	8.77	-0.90	-1.07	-0.94
6	January 2, 1992	February 1, 2000	2900	0.85	10.49	10.50	10.46	1.70	1.77	1.69
7	February 2, 2000	August 1, 2001	545	0.49	9.52	9.41	9.52	-0.97	-1.09	-0.95
8	August 2, 2001	January 1, 2006	1597	0.79	10.44	10.44	10.45	0.92	1.03	0.93
9	January 2, 2006	December 31, 2011	2162	0.83	9.89	9.91	9.90	-0.55	-0.53	-0.55
10	December 31, 2011	December 31, 2011	0	#N/A	#N/A	#N/A	#N/A	#N/A	#N/A	#N/A
Record	April 6, 1962	December 31, 2011	17727	1.03	9.68	9.74	9.69			

Title Sheet / ReleaseNotes / **TABLE** / BREAK POINTS / COMPUTATIONS / WATER-LEVEL DATA / Cum Z-Score Curve / Freq Curve

Figure 1-5.   Screen capture showing ZEBRA worksheet for tabulation of basic statistics for each cumulative water-level frequency distribution curve.